WHAT

EVERY WOMAN

SHOULD KNOW

WHAT
EVERY WOMAN
SHOULD KNOW
ABOUT A MAN

JAMES L. JOHNSON

ZONDERVAN
PUBLISHING HOUSE
OF THE ZONDERVAN CORPORATION
GRAND RAPIDS, MICHIGAN 49506

OTHER BOOKS BY JAMES L. JOHNSON

Code Name Sebastian

The Nine Lives of Alphonse

A Handful of Dominoes

A Piece of the Moon Is Missing

The Death of Kings

The Nine to Five Complex

Before Honor

Quotations from Charlotte Holt Clinebell abridged from pp. 23, 32, 33, 57, 60, 67, 61 of *Meet Me in the Middle* by Charlotte Holt Clinebell. Copyright © 1973 by Charlotte Holt Clinebell. Used by permission of Harper & Row, Publishers, Inc.

WHAT EVERY WOMAN SHOULD KNOW ABOUT A MAN

© 1977 by The Zondervan Corporation
Grand Rapids, Michigan

Library of Congress Cataloging in Publication Data
Johnson, James Leonard, 1927-
    What every woman should know about a man.

    1. Men.   2. Men—Psychology.   3. Marriage.   I. Title.
HQ1067.J64   301.41   77-1925

Second printing June 1977
ISBN 0-310-26620-3

Printed in the United States of America

To My Wife Rosemary
WHOSE LOVE ENCOURAGED ME
TO MAKE THIS JOURNEY

CONTENTS

AUTHOR'S ACKNOWLEDGMENTS

Special thanks to all those people who were willing to share their experiences candidly and from whom the major part of this book has been drawn. The names used in the case histories are fictional, but the experiences they represent are not.

Also to those professional people — the psychologists and ministers and counselors — who kindly consented to talk to me "off the cuff," without whom I could not have provided the analysis of the problems raised here, and who did it purely out of concern for what I was trying to communicate, I am and shall be eternally grateful.

Finally, I am indebted to those authors (and their publishers) quoted in this book who provided additional and invaluable insights and documentation from their special fields of counseling and professional disciplines.

PREFACE

I dare do all that may become a man;
Who dares do more is none.
                              — Shakespeare

It's tough to be a man. Despite what women claim of late — that the male animal has it all his own way and loves it — any honest man will readily confess that the masculine suit does not always fit well or comfortably. Tradition has handed him a suit of armor, in fact, an unyielding, inflexible, and often constricting mantle that cannot be stripped off without great cost to himself.

It is this "masculine armor" that plagues him, not so much in terms of whether he has "done more," but whether he has "done enough" to measure up to the mark. Or even more terrifying to him is the searching question as to whether he has "dared do all" that makes for manhood.

The anxiety begins as early as five years of age on the playground and remains until the last battle with death at seventy-five. During that span of years a man spends 75 percent of his lifetime at work, 15 percent with his family, and 10 percent on various recreational and leisure activities. Throughout all those years and activities he is driven to perform, to maintain an image of authority, stamina, courage, and decisiveness.

11

And then at seventy-five he makes his one final curtain call when all the vestiges of manhood are now reduced to a paltry sum of mere chemistry, most of which by then is fizzleless. And yet even in the act of dying, he will fight or "dare to do all" that becomes a man, even as he lived. Now it is to "die like a man" which, for some, means biting the bullet while reciting something from Kipling or the Psalms. For others, it is in the making of one last grand charge on the intravenous bottles and bedpan, those mocking elements that pose the final threat to the manly glands, hoping to go out in a blaze of glory, shouting "Jehoshaphat!" or a grand "Hallelujah!"

What a man was in life, as the myth has it, will be proven by the way he dies. For a man to whimper out his last moments in the confusion of pain is, as folklore has it, a poor epitaph to his manhood; and it says that he never really lived as a "true man" at all. His death proved that he would not "dare" do all that "becomes a man."

This, of course, is the myth conjured up in the halls of the military who have always put extreme emphasis on a "proper death in keeping with true manhood and that which will give glory to the corps." But even so, the question of a proper and true measurement of a man is as much the concern of women — or should be — as men. For it is the woman and her idealism about men that often will drive a man to try to live the myth, as Macbeth could strongly testify. And it is as much the concern of the Christian — perhaps even more so — as the non-Christian, because the definition of a "Christian man" can be often more complex.

At any rate, if a woman is to know what drives a man, then she must know the difference between the myth and the reality. There is that folklore that conjures up images of manhood in one dimension — which is mostly in the physical performance — but within that are the instinctual drives that man draws on for survival. It is not enough to tell a man to put aside the historical heroes of manhood as "myth," when in actuality he is driven by his own sense of psychological need to perform in like manner. The woman who demeans hero images that go with manhood complicates the issue at best.

In any case, there are those one-dimensional images of manhood that every man, rightly or wrongly, tries to fulfill as part of his sex role. To be a man is too often computed in terms of muscle and bone alone; it is John Wayne as "Rooster Cogburn" with a patch over his eye, shooting the bad guys out of their saddles and cursing each of them as they die; it is Muhammed Ali splattering Joe Frazer's nose to shreds while quoting free verse; it is Joe Namath on gimpy knees "standing in the pocket" and firing one more long bomb to victory; it is Hilliard climbing Everest, Patton roaring up the Rhine, Mark Spitz sporting gold medals, or George Wallace ruling Alabama from a wheelchair.

All of these images, of course, have their genuine ingredients that make for manhood. For as Montaigne put it, "Wherever a man strives for something and wins — or even loses — there is something akin to manhood there."

And yet despite the attempts of women's liberation to put down man as no higher than the sum of what a woman makes him, most women still cling to the traditional images of brawn as their ideal. True manhood is still linked to figures of physical dominance, commanding authority, exhibiting sheer strength of will and performances that demonstrate "true grit." Traditional literature, as well as the popular contemporary forms, maintain the James Bond types who master the universe with cunning, device, karate, and sexual virility. The women who chase them, idolize them, endorse them, want to love them, and adore the brute in them finally surrender to them for the mere thrill of being mastered. Advertising campaigns continue to reinforce that image; the perfect male is cast in terms of muscle-bulging athletes, hairy-chested actors, and superhuman military or space heroes who exhibit such immense physical power that thousands of women — literally or in their fantasies — flock to be touched by their shadow.

Of course, this may well be a part of manhood. But it is not the totality of it. For if pure muscle and bone are synonymous with manhood, then what is to be said for those who fought their wars on other fronts? What is to be said for the Einsteins, the Schweitzers, the Sibeliuses, the Michelangelos, who put their brains to work to build a scaffolding for man to climb up to new heights in science, art, philosophy, and religion? What is to be said for those who made their manliness work in debate in political, social, and religious arenas, their weapons being nothing more than mind and tongue and faith disciplined to fight the battles for those too poor to stand? What is to be said for these? Not much perhaps?

Maybe it's up to the woman today to become aware of these myths that drive her man to prove himself in ways that are "masculine." If it is true that it is a woman who makes the man or breaks him, then surely she would be wise in knowing the difference between the myth and the reality.

If a woman cares enough, she can come to know and recognize her man as a complicated species. To know him as one driven to reach the mark of manhood in the purely physical and psychological is to know the reason for sexual demands; it is then possible to know why he takes so much of an authoritarian stance; it is then more readily apparent why he insists on leading, making decisions, "doing it his way," controlling, demanding, and resisting any exchange of sex roles. To know a man, not simply on the surface, but to know what drives him from within, to know the reality of him apart from the myth, is to find peace and love with him and to share the immensity of his true strength.

If a man is a product of the myths that have been handed down from centuries past and that have conditioned him to act the way he does, the reality can come to him only when he sees it for what it is. It is the woman who often controls that — if she wants to, if she loves him enough, and if she is not herself controlled by the myths perpetuated about her own sex.

But the modern women's liberation movement has not encouraged or espoused this responsibility for women. In fact, for the most part, the female freedom movement has pushed man off the stage and stalled him in his quest for true self-identity. While women come to an understanding of themselves and grab onto their new roles as "free women," men are left floundering in their uncertainty as to what it all means to them. They are caught in the backwash, aware of the changes in women toward them, but now more concerned that any gestures they make in their manhood mean very little.

If it is true, then, as the psychologists claim, that the American male is experiencing more sexual impotency than ever before in history, it may be because he does not know how to handle the "equal time in bed" that is just one part of the feminine freedom movement. He is no longer the initiator of sex, but now must at the same time become the recipient of her sexual aggressions; it is not that he finds this so hard to take, but he does not know how to adjust to the change so quickly. It is this confusion between what the man has learned to fulfill as his proper role as a man and the new role of women that has left him feeling a loss of value. His only alternative then is to take absurd steps to reinforce his own image of male dominance.

This female freedom movement has gone so far in sowing confusion and perhaps even some terror in men that there has finally emerged a desperate counterpart to women's liberation called "The Society for Dirty Old Men." The main idea of this bizarre organization, according to Carol Leiman in an article in the *Chicago Tribune*, is to "keep women barefoot, pregnant and in some dirty old man's kitchen." The group claims 10,000 members in twenty-two states, and it's growing. David L. Palmer, the director, claims that "we were a major factor in defeating the passage of the Equal Rights Amendment in Indiana," and adds, "our real aim is to take a humorous approach to remedy the attitudes of society toward the older man [Palmer is an ancient 28], and we definitely believe in male supremacy."

All this says is that there is a tragic development of new tensions in the war of the sexes — the man seeking to dominate as he feels his manliness dictates and the woman seeking to be free of that domination. The war is really unnecessary, and if a woman would take the time to know her man apart from the traditional folklore, she would realize that he really does not want to be a muscle-bound, domineering, sexual maniac. Man, in other words, is more than a creature consumed by his appetite for sex, money, and power and the need to have his woman subservient to him. If she will find that out in him, perhaps he, likewise, will realize it himself. And both will become the richer for it.

Does this have anything to do with Christian man and his relationship to the Christian woman in his life?

Yes, as much and more.

For instance, a man who becomes a Christian does not always automatically unload the mythical dimensions that he feels must prove his manhood. Therefore, he may be slow to cleave to biblical images that seem far too genteel and muscleless and even come across as being "feminine." The presentation of Jesus in effeminate garb, the modifying of Christian behavior as summed up in the B-attitudes and the Sermon on the Mount, all make him feel somewhat uncomfortable and sometimes even "short-changed." Add to that the seemingly unchallenging church duty roster which confines itself to ushering, singing in the choir, taking up the offering, and driving the bus, and it is not surprising that he may miss a few Sundays in the sanctuary in favor of weekend fishing.

This does not mean he believes less or that he doubts the validity of Christianity or his own experience in redemption. It simply means that he is finding it difficult to reorient himself to the biblical measurement of a man. It means also that perhaps church leadership, who interpret biblical images in terms that do not challenge manhood or provide masculine behavioral models, need to take a second look at their ministry. It at least explains why even a Christian man will gorge himself on TV football, hockey, or any "contact" sport where he can vicariously enter into what is "combat suitable for a man." And what this does say, without question, is that his wife should be aware of this conflict within him and not charge his absence from church or his occasional indifference as rejection of Christianity.

After all, when the world puts its stock in generals and clean-up hitters, rallies to Evel Knievel in his mad motorcycle jumps, and seeks to match Jimmy Connors on the tennis court, it is understandably difficult for a man to sing out with gusto, "O Day of Re and Gladness."

The Christian man must learn to know himself, find himself, come to grips afresh and anew with the biblical concept of manliness. He must realize that the Bible does not present a "lesser man," nor is the "new man" in Christ for service at the altar only and not for combat in the world. Until he does, however, there is often a state of tension with his Christian wife. Not that he blames her. He just yearns to "break out" of the sanctuary now and then and "do his thing." In other words, he wants to "dare do all that may become a man."

When Dietrich Bonhoeffer finally left his pulpit and joined the German underground to resist Hitler, he did so out of a conviction that only by such resistance could the monstrous Third Reich be ended. He may not have done that to prove his manhood, but the act he chose, to him at any rate, was more "manly" and godlike than taking a pose of submission to evil. It is for this reason he wrote:

> The church must get out of the cloister and into the world . . .
> man is challenged to participate in the sufferings of God at the
> hands of a godless world. He must therefore plunge himself

into the life of a godless world without attempting to gloss over its ungodliness with a veneer of religion or trying to transfigure it . . . to be a Christian does not mean to be religious in a particular way, to cultivate some form of asceticism . . . but to be a man.[1]

A Christian man will identify with that statement. The theologians may argue Bonhoeffer's theology or his action that led him to the underground resistance movement; but for a man who drinks his coffee straight, does his fifty pushups every morning, and goes out into his own "jungle" every day to engage in what is often a war of economic and moral survival, it's probably the proper and only way to go.

Jesus' journey to the cross, Paul's gutsy drive through Asia to proclaim Christ, and the record of those church fathers who put their necks on the block for Christian conviction — to say nothing of the modern martyrs — carry the same element of manliness. With that in mind, it is incumbent on those who communicate Christian history to declare them and the events they affected.

So until he recognizes that the proof of his manliness may not be in terms of great muscular performances, that there are varied measurements of manhood spiritually and otherwise, the Christian man will have to be indulged to some degree. That may mean a wife may have to spend some Sundays in church by herself; she may go to prayer meeting while he plays football or watches it; she may go to the youth banquet while he goes bowling. But that need not be the basis for divorce, nor should she conclude that he is no longer interested in spiritual things because he does so.

These are some of the conflicts this book deals with that, hopefully, will help women who are "bewitched, bothered, and bewildered" about their men. For while the women are caught between the traditional, biblical role of submission to their men and the pressure of independent liberation philosophy, they must at the same time maintain some order in themselves and in their relationships with their men. Much has been said about what women need in their pursuit of totality and fulfillment as individuals, wives, and mothers. Now it is time women realize that a man is not simply a composite of bursting glands who must be satisfied at every urge and who can be possessed only as he is satisfied that way. These are the "surface" things; they do not constitute the totality of a man, the inner feelings, yearnings, longings, secret fears, weaknesses, or anxieties.

The Christian woman who will take time to recognize this inner area of the man in her life — the loneliness, the fear, and the desire to be loved and even protected despite his pose of self-sufficiency and command — will be wiser and much more fulfilled in her relationship with him. The Christian man, likewise, who will take the time to reexamine himself in terms of his manhood, both from the mythical, traditional measurements and from that which is Christian, can perhaps better understand himself. If he does, he is going to be a far better husband and a far better man in the truest sense.

Finally, this book is not written as a psychologist's manual on man-woman relationships, nor does it espouse in any way the "keys to successful marriage." This is a journalist's view of the problem, a composite of many interviews with men — and women — over a period of five years. It is simply a look inside as it were. Though there are suggestions included about the solution to the problems as pertaining to man, they come from what people have experienced and proven in their lives and not from some clinical formulas.

What this book seeks to do, the author hopes, is to bring a new awareness of man, the reason he acts the way he does, something of his behavior, and what accounts for it. A lot of it may not be new. But much of it should be said again — and again. At any rate, the author hopes that whatever does come through will be viewed as what other people have shared, experienced, and laid hold of to salvage shaky marriages. Through that perhaps someone will find a new level of relationship with that man in her life, and hopefully the man who reads it will find himself and be led to share more of himself with his wife.

It is the author's conviction that only through this renewal can many of the fragmented marriages be saved and the destructive presumptions of the single be corrected. It may be asking too much, but perhaps the Body collectively will come to a new realization that there is much ground yet to possess in this whole area of Christian interpersonal relationships.

WHAT
EVERY WOMAN
SHOULD KNOW
ABOUT A MAN

1.

WHAT SHE
MAY THINK
MAY BE FOLLY

I have no other but a woman's reason;
I think him so, because I think him so.

— Shakespeare

Marilyn R. is thirty-four years old and in a wheelchair. She will be in it until she dies. She is suffering from multiple sclerosis and has been that way for six years. Her home during those six years has been a small bedroom in a nursing home; her daily recreation has been to wheel herself down the long, dim corridor where the images of broken humanity are everywhere, like herself — some in wheelchairs, others hobbling on crutches, and still others half crawling their last mile to death.

For six years, every day, except for illnesses and other emergencies — which have been rare — her husband, Ron, aged thirty-six, has been there to wheel her to the cafeteria for lunch. Every night at 6:30 he is there for dinner.

Marilyn and Ron have been married ten years. They have had only four "normal" years together. There is no "sane" reason in terms of today's marriage commitments, as the world defines them, for Ron to continue to carry that burden. There is no logic in how a relationship like that continues when it is so limited in what each can give to the other, sexually or in any other area of communication. Nobody knows how Ron can continue day after day, night after night, in his lonely world under the pressures for the kind of companionship he needs and, as the world would put it, "deserves."

There are days when Marilyn senses the incongruity of the relationship, and through her tears she pleads with him. "You're losing out," she says. "I'm as good as dead; in fact, most of me *is* dead as far as being anything to you is concerned. I would rather die, God surely knows it. But until He releases me from this prison, there is no reason for you to keep coming here all the time, because you know there is no hope for me . . . and none for you . . . you've got every legitimate ground to go out and find someone else to live with, someone you can relate to, someone you can love and find fulfillment with. . . ."

Ron has listened to her pleadings patiently, but he has not yielded. "I love you, honey," he says, as he has always said, and he touches her cheeks gently with his fingers, stroking away the tears. "It hasn't changed because you are sick. My needs are met in being with you. That's all that matters."

A few houses from Ron's place is the palatial residence of Walter L. He is a successful publisher of religious books, a person who has practiced efficiency, order, and command, topped off by a high-speed turbine kind of drive. He is athletic, a great tennis player, a former fighter pilot in World War II. His world is one of those where everything is, and must be, perfectly synchronized — everything in place, everything done as he expects when he expects. Walter is chairman of the board of elders of his church, and he runs the church board as he does his own publishing house and his own family, with the same drive and demands. He is a "man's man," in every sense.

His wife, Gladys, is a quiet, unassuming, obedient, and attractive person — she knows she must continue to keep up that appearance to complement her husband's aura of success — but she often looks pale, even exhausted. She has borne Walter five sons, all normal. For twenty-four years she has lived with this "literal whirlwind" of a husband. She has yielded to his every demand, "as a good wife should," his every whim, his every order for perfection.

Walter makes love to Gladys as fiercely as he drives his staff or smashes his way through a tennis game, as if somehow he is striving to be the crown of all manhood; and she takes it, even when she does not feel like returning it in kind.

Gladys has only one creeping sense of resistance, and that is the thought of another fifteen years of the same thing — living with the roaring, charging, galloping man who is her husband. It does not mean she loves him less. But she desperately wants one thing: "If I could only have him stand still in the middle of the room for just five minutes and allow him to see that the world is fixed, in place, that it needs no repair, that God has some parts of it under His own control. If for one night we could lie in bed next to each other and take a quiet fifteen minutes to read, to forget just once that bed is only for sex. If I could just have some kind of conversation with him about anything, any dumb thing. What is there in such a man that won't let his brain stop whirling, his muscles stop twitching, his virile sap stop flowing?"

While Gladys ponders that with a kind of hopeless resignation, a few blocks from her another drama is unfolding. Charlie W. is after that raccoon again. Only this time he is chasing it across his roof — that new roof he himself put on last year — with a fishing net in his hands. Charlie W. is about to "get that varmint once and for all before she raises a family under my front porch." Raccoons, however, still have the edge on man when it comes to agility and strategy, and Charlie finds it out one minute later. There is a wild sweep of the fishing net, a sudden teetering, a wild yell, a long, ominous sliding sound, and a final thump as he hits the ground twelve feet below.

As the ambulance carries Charlie away to put his broken leg in a cast, his wife, Mary, simply stands in the driveway and shakes her head, as she has been shaking it for thirteen years of her life with Charlie. "There's an Animal Control Center four blocks away where men are trained to catch raccoons," she says to a sympathetic neighbor in a tone of disbelief. "Yet my husband, that gloriously flat-footed, high-wire actor has to make his own dive again. Did you ever see such a man as mine? He has to cut down his own trees, because tree surgeons are hackers, not cutters; he does his own plumbing that floods us out, builds his own garage that leaks; he even climbs his own flagpole to put a ball on top to make it complete. Do you know how much he has paid in hospital bills in thirteen years just to prove he could do it all himself? Is he doing some kind of penance? For what? Isn't there an easier way for a man to make his day go?"

Mary says it half laughingly, trying to toss it all aside as humorous. But inside there is some genuine bafflement, even frustration, with those repeated experiences of a man who seems bent on doing himself in.

Even Gladys can rationalize the commando husband she has with a philosophical "Oh, well" kind of resignation. And from that point she will begin dutifully to check off his good points and conclude that maybe he isn't so demanding a man that she can't abide him. But inwardly, she will experience that same sense of gnawing questioning, that heavy hand of "Does it have to be this way all the time?"

Only Marilyn vents her feelings honestly because there is no reason for pretense, nor is there time to deal in facades or cover-ups. Yet in her desire that Ron be set free from her there is still a gross misunderstanding of him, of his loyalty which she cannot comprehend as true love.

These are but a few illustrations that point up the confusion of women over what makes their particular men tick. In a sense, they represent an increasingly common bewilderment due to the blind spots women have about men in general. Since Cleopatra made her famous statement about Antony — and even before that — that he "is at best a conundrum of conundrums," women have agreed silently and vocally.

Fortunately the tension factors that lie in the subsurface areas of these three marriages can be controlled within the values of Christian experience. But this is not a guarantee in every marriage. Irritations and frustrations stemming from women's inability to understand their men can corrode emotions to the breaking point. True, a great number of wives today have learned to laugh off the problems, resign themselves to them, and adjust to the peculiarities of male behavior. But increasingly, and alarmingly so, there are those tragic separations between Christian husband and wife who, rather than adjust or draw on their faith or lean on their vows of love, choose to go their separate ways. The reasons are not all the same, and statistics show that more men than women instigate the divorces. But with the growing feminist liberation movement, the door has been sprung open to encourage more women to make the break. Much of the time, the separation is a result of a total misunderstanding of their husbands — their drives, the roles they play, the peculiar chemistry that makes them what they are and which often then labels them "conundrums."

Equally as tragic as divorce, however, is the state of "uncertain union" which a man and a woman can maintain together under the same roof, each unable or unwilling to share those subsurface confusions about the other. Many a woman like Gladys has suffered in obedient silence for twenty-four years with her "Walter," believing that it is her "spiritual duty," rather than risk honest communication. Many a woman like Mary has repressed resentment at the "high jinks" of her Charlie, preferring to unload it on a neighbor or a friend but never really desiring or daring to ask the same questions of him.

These dark corners of the Christian marriage remain so because the woman is never quite sure how her husband will receive her expressions of her fears, frustrations, irritations, or confusions. Meanwhile, these repressions, no matter how small, continue to dig insidiously at the core of the relationship, bending the fragile straws of that union — sometimes to the breaking point.

Women who give up finally and go through the torment of separation or else grit their teeth in determination to make the best of it are plagued by that one nagging question: *What makes a man as he is?* Too many women have lost their sense of the ideal which they had when they married; instead, they are now confronted with the different sides of their man, the peculiarities of behavior they never thought he could assume, the annoying habits, the strange fixations about dominance and combative activities, and the frustrating unpredictableness of him. Some of this ought to be expected, of course, since there are departures from the ideal that show up on both sides with the passage of time, and many women accept the changes stoically or find that love does conquer all — or at least provides a decent truce in the conflicts. Others, though, find them to be annoyances that grow into a psychological pressure which finally spills over into the union itself.

Marriage counselors, and even anthropologists who have

studied man from the early Neanderthals on, are not sure they can put together a diagram of man that will account for all the mysteries resident there. Yet it is reasonable to assume that if women would get some insight early in life as to why a man behaves as he does — at least in general terms of masculinity — what peculiar mechanisms drive him internally, whether it be glandular, chemical, chromosonal, or that he was loved too much or not enough by his mother — there would be a lessening of tension and a saving of marriages.

Interestingly enough, sex does not play as big a part in the tensions that strike the Christian marriage as is believed. Though "sexual incompatibility" is often cited in divorce suits or in defining the stresses and strains within a union, most of the time the sex problem is tied to something already gone awry elsewhere in that union.

To prove this is not an exaggeration, here are a few cases selected from the many that illustrate the point:

Case 1: "He resents my education and the fact that it could really make me independent of him economically if I wanted to be. I guess he is threatened by equality on this level. And so he keeps putting me down in front of my friends. Now it has become a tension factor that is beginning to affect other areas of our married life."

Case 2: "He has slipped into a state of continual moodiness, a constant downer almost. I made a graph of his moods in a typical month in the last year, and they look like a stock market plunge in 1929. He comes home, eats — mostly in silence — gets to his favorite chair in front of the TV, and stays there until after the ten o'clock news. Then he's off to bed, and I am left with battening down the kids and any hatches still open in the house. By the time I get to bed, he is long gone to dreamland. Our spiritual life, along with everything else, is sliding off the edge too. I keep trying to get him to open up to me, tell me why he is in the deeps, but it only seems to antagonize him. Sometimes I wonder if this is all there is for the next thirty years."

Case 3: "For me, it's too much sex from him; he demands it all the time with no thought of my feelings. I don't know how many women are awakened at all hours of the night by their husbands who are gripped with the urge, but it has about exhausted me. I am never asked, of course, never presumed to have feelings that need to be aroused. The demands in bed are matched by his demands in everything else; I feel like a glorious or not-so-glorious mechanized maid living with him merely to fulfill his every whim, urge, and caprice. Maybe that's what a good wife is supposed to do. But sometimes I feel frightened by what's happening . . . I'm afraid I'll get desperate and break with him . . . yet I know God put us together . . . so one has to hang on and hope, always hope."

Case 4: "He's too dependent on me. It should be the other way around in my book. But I am making the decisions he should be making about our finances, our children, just about everything. I find myself motivating him for his job, when he should be motivating me for mine in raising our children. It seems our roles are changing, and that is beginning to make me lose respect for him. I keep asking him to take command as the man of the house, but that only increases the tension. I still love him, of course, but maybe not the same as when we courted. I wish I knew why he needs to lean on me so much . . . and I hope that it won't ruin what feeling I have for him."

Case 5: "We have grown apart spiritually for some reason. I am in church activities all the time, Bible studies, children's work, but he has little interest in these things it seems. We don't have family devotions as we used to, though he at least drops a perfunctory prayer before meals. He goes to church, but he's antsy the whole hour he's there. He lives for his hunting, fishing, and bowling. I keep telling him there are more important things in life, such as the work of God. Our loss of communication in spiritual things seems to be cutting into other areas of our marriage. Sometimes he seems totally disinterested in his sex with me, and I wonder if I have lost my appeal to him. Where we once discussed spiritual things as the hub around which our values spun, now we argue about them, and sometimes he won't even talk about them. The gap is widening between us, and all the counseling in the world doesn't seem to change it."

Case 6: "He's gone all the time. He throws himself at every community challenge posed to him. He volunteers for everything, from heading the heart association to being a fireman. I get dragged along with him, but somehow I can't get ecstatic about building tot lots for the Jaycees or riding in the turret of a tank for the Fourth of July parade honoring the VFW. And riding a fire truck is not exactly ladylike either.

"Sure, it's funny in a way, and I try to laugh it off — and succeed most of the time. And I have to keep prodding him to pay attention to his home life a little more. But he sees me as keeper of the home and the children while he is the keeper of the community fires. We spend less and less time together. He eats and runs. Lately he isn't even eating at home. I figure I am running a boardinghouse for him, bed and board which has now become 'bed and bored.' I don't want him to become a stranger to me. I pray he won't."

Cast 7: "He always felt totally inadequate sexually, from the very first night. In the years since it has played on him so much that now he has become neurotic over it. Psychotherapy doesn't help much, and there is nothing wrong with him physically. True, I have always been more forward than he, taking much of the responsibility; but I don't think that seems to be the problem, though I am not sure. I don't think I demand that much in sex, and I keep telling him that. Now I wonder if there isn't something wrong with me. Sometimes I ask him to pray with me just before getting into bed; but it is a bit awkward to ask a man to share my prayer about his becoming sexually adequate tonight. It's even a little bizarre and makes him more tense. I've read everything on the subject of what a woman should expect in sex from a man; I've read a lot of that to him too, but it doesn't help. I wonder sometimes if I should slip him one of those illustrated books like *The Joy of Sex* or something; maybe that would get him in the mood more often. Meanwhile I tell myself I can live without it. But I wonder if *he* can. His failure in sex has given him a sense of inferiority in everything else, even his job. I just have to keep telling God to help me hang on . . . help him hang on . . . that there has to be an answer sooner or later."

The question these cases suggest is that favorite column in the woman's magazine: CAN THIS MARRIAGE BE SAVED? More important, can Christianity provide the solutions to people caught in the impasses of these kinds of disbalanced unions? Is the problem going to create a hopeless gap between the partners? Is the only answer divorce?

Or does it mean that the woman might have to reexamine the peculiar make-up or mixture of molecules called man? Are there some secrets a woman ought to know, so that in the knowing she might find new approaches that will make the relationship work?

2.

THIS MUCH
SHE OWES

A woman moved is like a fountain troubled,
Muddy, ill-seeming, thick, bereft of beauty.
Such duty as the subject owes the prince,
Even such a woman oweth to her husband.

— Shakespeare

"Do you know what you snore like?" she asked upon awakening. It was still dark outside.

"I have never tuned in," he said.

"It sounds like something between a gargle and a sneeze."

"I will retune my sinuses. Incidentally, your rendition sounds like wild geese calling — "

"I don't snore."

"How do you know?"

"Because I know."

"Why don't you wake up some night and listen?"

"I couldn't hear it over yours."

"Well, maybe I've got a hole, like a whale, on the top of my head, hidden under my hair somewhere. I'll try plugging up the hole tonight, okay?"

"Plug the nose while you're at it. It's all in your nose."

"Plug the nose and it will come out my ears. Then what?"

"Heaven forbid. The size of those ears?"

"I will wear a face mask and a snorkel tonight. How's that?"

"Don't be silly. Why do men have to snore like that?"

"What other men have you heard lately? We have only one male cat in the house — "

"I heard my father snore . . . just like yours."

"Well, I have someone in my corner at least."

"I mean it. There has to be a way a man can control his breathing while he sleeps so that he doesn't keep the rest of the house awake."

"Try sleeping yourself . . . you'll never notice it, only me . . . and if we can both pass out at the same time — "

"You can't time that so precisely, you know."

"Well, then, separate bedrooms may be the only answer — "

"You'd like that, I suppose?"

"What I'd like is a cup of coffee."

"And another thing . . . do all men leave their shoes by the bed with their socks in them?"

"Well, look at it this way . . . I'll be wearing brown again today . . . brown socks await me in the brown shoes. Saves you straining with the laundry."

"Who said I was straining?"

"Because there are no fresh, clean, brown socks in the drawer."

"I wash every week — "

"Except my socks . . . now how about that coffee?"

"You'll find the coffee ready . . . in the can."

"All things of gourmet delight are in cans in this house."

"That's unfair."

"But accurate, right?"

"Let's quit playing McMillan and wife, shall we?"

"McMillan had a maid. His wife was useless to him in the things that matter."

"Coffee?"

"Coffee at 5:30 in the morning, yes."

"Well, why not hire a maid then?"

"Just be one more to snore in this house," he said, slowly rising out of bed.

"Poor man."

"There are some who agree with you."

"What's that supposed to mean?"

"That a man denied his coffee made by his wife is a man suffering the ravages of poverty."

"Highly melodramatic — "

"But good, wouldn't you say? In any case, the point remains, I am the only man on this block who gets his coffee in the drugstore across from the station."

"You're the only man who gets up at the unearthly hour of 5:30 to shave, shower, and put on those same socks and shoes you wore yesterday."

"And I am the only man who works until 8:00 at night to bring home the necessary bread to maintain our little house, the cat, parakeet, and two lovely daughters — "

"You don't have to work that late. You *want* to work that late. You are a glutton for persecution. You don't want to be home with us for meals at a decent hour. You go out of here when it's dark and come home when it's dark. I haven't seen you in the daylight for five years — "

"My nose has grown a little longer and my chin is beginning to sag, but other than that there's no difference," and he stumbled over his shoes on the way out of the bedroom in the darkness.

"You could change into Rumpelstiltskin and I'd never know it," she insisted.

"Consider yourself spared," as he bumped into the bedroom door. "Who closed the door?"

"I did. At least in sleep one should have some privacy."

"There's only the cat to invade it — "

"When you make the coffee, make enough for me," she said as he moved into the bathroom.

"I'll also make one for the cat . . . he's taking a liking to sharing a saucer of Folger's with me every morning. He makes a great breakfast companion too — "

"You're digging at me again — "

"It has never worked before. I don't expect it will now."

"Watch how you squeeze the toothpaste, will you?"

"Is there an instruction manual?"

"I just don't want it squeezed from the middle."

"How about the Charmin?"

"Don't get cheeky with me," she called from the bedroom. "And don't get shaving cream on the mirror either."

"Why don't I take a pan of water out to the patio picnic table and shave there? I can't possibly hit the house from that distance —"

"And will you please put the toilet seat down? What is there about a man that he always has to leave the toilet seat up? Don't you figure anyone else uses the bathroom in this house?"

"The cat, of course —"

"It's not funny!"

"What is at 5:30 in the morning?"

Silence. Thus endeth the opening of the day for one man and his wife. Nothing really serious going on there. A lot of snappy banter, nothing more. At least not yet. This is the sixth year of those 5:30 A.M. dialogues. At first, in a big double bed, it was the murmurings and wonder of rising together. Then the twin beds, so the wife could get relief from the "heavy breathing" of his sleep that turned to snores. Since then the dialogue has become sharper, still played lightly or forced to a tone of lightness, but carrying the elements of innuendo. That will become sharper until it becomes bitter stabs at each other, until finally a year later there won't be any conversation at 5:30 in the morning. He will get up quietly, shower and shave quietly, and leave the house to get his breakfast at that lonely diner across from the station. Eighteen months later they will separate on her grounds of "incompatibility," meaning that he snored too much, did not squeeze the toothpaste tube right, and got shaving cream on the mirror. A cup of coffee in the morning — maybe that would have saved it. Who knows?

This is a case out of the secular arena, but there are like tensions in Christian marriages. Maybe a cup of coffee wasn't really the whole reason. Maybe that coffee was just a part of the larger fragments of discord swirling around both of them. The need for a cup of coffee when he gets up seems all too simple an issue for a man to get tight about anyway. But some men are like that. There are some things a man lives by, things he reaches for as symbols of order and love in his life. If they are missing, no matter how small they may appear to a wife, it can dig at him slowly and finally demoralize him. He comes to envy other men who get their coffee at home, who aren't nagged over the small stuff. He will fight to save what he has at home regardless, because a man hungers for continuity and hates to lose in anything related to it. The tragedy too often is that he does. And his wife loses with him.

To such a man, perhaps Shakespeare's *Romeo and Juliet* offers a bitter line:

> Romeo, come forth; come forth, thou fearful man:
> Affliction is enamoured of thy parts,
> And thou art wedded to calamity.

In the Christian situation, fortunately, there is some built-in gyro that keeps a marriage on course despite the tensions. But that gyro has to be reset now and then to be sure it is taking the union in the right direction. None of the women in the case histories noted in the last chapter sued for divorce or were sued by their husbands. At least not yet. The seeds of testiness may be there, however, ready to produce the ugly thorns of irritation which can cause irreconcilable differences (if there can be such a term for Christian people).

It would seem, then, that in the cases referred to there should be answers within reach to head off any disaster. If not on the human level, certainly in the wealth of spiritual resources available to the Christian. But again the confusions and let-downs a woman experiences with a man — which sometimes begin with the little irritations about his sloppy habits — and the complications that develop out of them are not always so easily answered by prayer or biblical principles. It takes patience and perseverance and faith and commitment on both sides to make the spiritual resources work. And certainly true love. At the same time, the Christian value system was not designed to give answers as to why man is the way he is, though certainly the heart of it does urge patience to pursue them. Christianity works, after all, only as people are willing to exercise their faith together that God will enable them to overcome the rough edges and know healing and restoration.

It must be emphasized again, however, that in many instances the tension factors are rooted mainly in a failure to understand what man is like — what he *really* is versus the mythical image he holds about himself and which many women conjure up about him. Because he acts in certain ways that are unreasonable or because he may too often appear distant does not mean that he has lost interest in his wife or that he is so "pigheaded" that he won't listen to honest appeals. Most of the time, he does not even realize he is that way; or sometimes, if he does sense it, he will charge it up to the peculiar chemistry that is his as a man.

Perhaps in this regard the church needs to consider more seriously a proper orientation into the man-woman mystique that would prepare couples for the intimacies and conflicts of courtship and marriage. But more than that, there is a desperate need for awareness of the distinctive differences between a man and a woman other than the biological. Little, if anything, is taught in terms of the human conflicts that can emerge in a lifetime with another person; nor is there any preparation for coping with those changes in personality, behavior, or habits that irritate and chafe. The sudden realization that her "shining knight" of courtship days really wears long underwear is a bit shocking to any woman. Marriage is brutally exposing, and idealism must give way to reality. The ability to come to terms with that reality is the key to a successful marriage, and sometimes the woman finds the strain a bit more difficult.

The church's attitude that God's will for two people coming together is insurance that it will succeed does not carry far enough. This does not negate the concern of God that the union succeed. But there is a false presumption in it that says, "Let the union find its own course, let it emerge naturally, let the two people involved find their own levels with each other, and God will take care of the tension factors." Case histories do not bear this out, unfortunately. What God is willing to do, as the experience of many proves, is provide the value system — that is, the worth of individuals — that will bring honesty and openness to each other. But both those people must appropriate the value system in its totality and have faith in it, if God is going to enter into the relationship.

The premarital counseling that simply concentrates on Ephesians 5 — husbands "love" and wives "obey" — does not allow for the many intricacies of personality and human weakness that can become blown out of proportion. Yes, love does work to blind the eyes to the shortcomings and irritations of the other; obedience of a wife does lead her to accept a role stoically and with resignation, despite the inner confusions and tensions she has about the way her husband is, or acts, or whatever.

But love can erode under pressure, disappointment, or disillusionment. And obedience is a yoke that hangs heavy when the mind ponders in some terror, "Just what kind of man is he after all?" A marriage union is delicate at best, and what cracks it often is this area of misunderstanding of each other. The woman who is not prepared, beyond the love and obedience compulsions, to reconcile those attributes that run cross-grain is a woman who takes a long time to come to grips, and sometimes there just isn't the patience to endure long enough. And if it is the woman who can, as Shakespeare put it, "sing the savageness out of a bear," then she must know a bit more about that "bear" if her song is to be successful.

Because of this lack of a solid approach to the man-woman relationship (women have made their case in over forty books on the subject to date), the norm for Christian young people has come down to the purely sexual. For the woman, then, as the world teaches, the man is the aggressor, the grand strategist who will use every device to get one thing from her. The woman can entice him, teach him, hold him off, until she can trade off her sexual attractiveness for a compact of marriage. Whatever problems might emerge later can always be solved in bed. This worldly concept regarding marriage, if allowed to stand without a proper countering by the church with regard to higher human values, will breed a future generation of torn-up Christian families.

It is not unusual to find young people on Christian campuses who have taken on the world's slogan, "If you can make out good in bed, everything else is an afterthought." The woman learns to "keep him satisfied sexually, give in when he asks, and everything will fall into place." This is the greatest delusion ever perpetrated about the marriage union, and it is the greatest single misunderstanding women can entertain about men. Actually, in the cases of Ron, Gladys, and Mary there were no sexual crises as such, except that Gladys felt used by her demanding husband rather than complemented. In the other cases referred to earlier, only two women confessed problems in the sex area, but these were tied to other problem situations.

In examining divorce cases in one Midwestern city, divorces among Christians that is, a Christian lawyer stated that most of his cases were not due to breakdowns in sexual relations. Rather, as he put it, "These couples confessed that their sex life was normal and in some instances terrific. The problem really came down to an inability to communicate outside the bed. Sex was expected to cover for the broken bridges in the many other areas of the daily communication exchange. When communication is lost in the hours of the day outside bed, sex ultimately is reduced to a desperate function, a feeble and all too brief attempt to find the answers to what is missing."

The cruelest form of "panacea" suggested in all the books on sex, most Christian ones included, is that a man simply needs to be "turned on" sexually by his wife to dissolve any serious problems in the relationship. Although women should learn what that appeal can do, too many wives have swallowed this view and adopted an out-of-character burlesque approach to her man only to find him really *turned off* by it and even embarrassed. Which says that not all men react the same way to those deliberate overtures. When one woman tried the idea of wrapping herself in nothing but Saran Wrap to greet her husband at the door, his first reaction was simply, "Isn't that a little expensive for what you had in mind?"

What this does is destroy further the woman's sense of self-worth and self-image, and the rejection complicates the marriage even more. Often the woman sets this kind of sexual encounter deliberately as if it is the key to the missing link in the relationship, when all the man really wants is a quiet time of small talk with her.

Yet little of this is taught to Christian women, any more than Christian men are instructed about the real needs of a woman. The secular world does more on this subject perhaps; there unfortunately marriage is becoming simply a matter of convenience, to last only as long as there is continuing sexual compatibility. But the Christian marriage involves more than that; it simply must. It is a display case for God, for one thing. It cannot be the "inevitable endurance" of a woman making it somehow with a man, or a man tolerating a woman merely for the sake of Christianity. It must be a finely tuned relationship, where both seek to know and understand each other and face their problems openly and honestly. If Christian marriage comes to that "impossible area" where it can no longer work, where two people don't want to bother with it, then it becomes more and more impossible to lend credibility to the Christian position on the value and endurance of interpersonal relationships.

Meanwhile, however, the emphasis on the human sexual apparatus instead of on human behavior, as the modern sexologist view has it, is developing in Christian young people, from early adolescents on, the seeds of immaturity linked to ignorance that are bound to lead to serious conflicts in marriage.

"Sex has become," as Aldous Huxley once put it, commenting on this trend, "a maniac struggling in the musky darkness with another maniac."

And as Joseph Epstein put it in his book *Divorced in America: Marriage in an Age of Possibility:*

> Where once Bertrand Russell stood, knight of scientific reason in constant combat with unnecessary human cruelty, believer in sexual liberation, but always within standards of decency and consideration for others, now stands the clinicians of genitalia, eyes to camera lens, electronic equipment plugged in, making ready still another blow by blow account of the clitoris or prostate in action.[1]

No, sex and its role is only one part of the man-woman relationship, and though it is important, a woman needs to know that man has other dimensions equally as critical to his well-being. It is not simply that a man wants or needs a sex partner for forty years and nothing more, as Ron proved with Marilyn.

Marilyn, even in her last dying breath with Ron faithfully at her side, could still not understand how he could remain faithful to her for six years without any sexual expression between them. She had failed to understand that he had a love for her that ran deeper than that.

Gladys did not find out about her Walt either, until a stroke paralyzed him at fifty-five years of age, in his prime. Now that he is helpless and fading slowly from life, a man who finally is "standing still long enough to know that the world is fixed and in place," Gladys has come to understand him. She knows now the real fragility of that "roaring, galloping, whirlwind of a man" who used all of that to cover an almost childlike need to be loved and accepted. To come to an understanding of Walter at this point is a little late, however, because he is now beyond the point of wanting to be understood.

Mary never did find out about her Charlie — even though she could have asked him — because before she could get up the courage to question him as to why he had to perform like a "clown in a three-ring circus all the time," he died when a heavy tractor he insisted on driving to help a friend fell over on him. Hers, perhaps, is the greater agony — never to have known what was in Charlie that made him want to "perform," to do it himself. Never to know that in him was that same "call of the wild" that drove Hillary to climb Everest, that compelled Lindberg to fly the Atlantic alone, that sent John Glenn into space. If she had known, maybe she would have experienced much more love and peace in her fourteen years with Charlie.

It does not take a practicing psychologist to understand what makes a man tick. A woman who loves her man enough to want to know can know. If love is there, communication is available. A man doesn't always understand why he is what he is either, but a powerful lot of understanding comes through when both husband and wife try to find out together. When that knowledge comes through, even in small pieces, perhaps the breaking points that have destroyed marriages need not materialize.

God does have a stake, a high one, in the lives of His own. It is worth it for a woman, now that she has made her case for herself over and over again for the benefit of man, to know about her man. God's desire is for love, harmony, understanding, and communication. But He leaves that to His own to pursue and work out.

Meanwhile, not far across town from Marilyn's hospital, and Walter's palatial palace, and Charlie's "gymnastic arena" (as Mary called it), two young people stand before the altar ready to exchange their vows. Douglas L. and Midge R. are about to begin what is either going to be a short, jerky, painful life of "unholy" matrimony or an incredible, exciting journey of fulfillment and reward.

As has been true since the beginning of time, the future of that marriage rests more heavily on Midge and her understanding or lack of understanding of the tall, blond Adonis standing beside her. Does she know enough about him? Does he know enough about her? Committed Christians as they are, they have more going for them in the years ahead than those who are not. But even with that, will they be ready to accept the "thousand shocks that man and woman are heir to"? In short, can they make it?

3.

IN THE

BEGINNING . . .

An unlessoned girl, unschooled, unpractised;
Happy in this, she is not yet so old
But she may learn.

— Shakespeare

"What is your view of canonicity?"

Pause. "Of . . . what?"

"Canonicity . . . the continuity of the books of the Bible, their origin, their selection . . . you know."

"Well . . . I . . . I know there are sixty-six books in the Bible."

"But what is the peculiar mystery of the relationship of those books?"

Pause. Try a short laugh. Maybe he's really not serious. "You mean how were they inspired?"

"Something like that." He does not laugh.

They are parked in his VW in the community park near the lagoon. There are still mosquitoes in late September. A walk would be better, just to keep the bugs away. She has been slapping at them for most of the hour they have been sitting here. The conversation has moved from eschatology to the errors of TM to the Greek renderings of Paul's "love" appeal in 1 Corinthians 13. Now it has come back to canonicity. Midge R. is not against theology or the discussion of the Bible. It's just that this date with this man has been on that subject for four hours. Right now she would like a hamburger and a change of atmosphere that might get them on some new subject. She is not a scholar in theology, though she has had theology courses in college. She is an art major. He is not an artist, but that doesn't matter; he doesn't have to talk art. But she wishes he would not conclude that she is a theologian and would try to find some neutral ground.

So now he is going on with his careful analysis of biblical inspiration. She keeps looking across the lagoon to the McDonald's sign. She nods her head now and then to let him know she is there and listening — at least partially. But she would very much like that hamburger. He keeps his hands, both of them, firmly fixed on the steering wheel as if he were driving his way through 3,000 years of biblical history. He is kind of a nice guy, Midge concludes, but he is uncomfortable, as if he would like to change the subject. Maybe he keeps talking because he doesn't know what to do with his hands or is afraid what they'll do if they come off that wheel. Because he seems a bit nervous about that, she's feeling nervous and getting more hungry. She wishes he would relax, let go of that wheel, and ease up on his feet that are pushed tight on the clutch and brake, because his knees are jammed up against the steering wheel. A Volkswagen, she concludes, is not the place for a 6'5" guy to be talking to a girl on canonicity.

It is now after ten, and there is an 11:00 curfew at the dorm. That means he will have to move soon. After four hours of this, she would welcome the dorm, and she is sad that she feels that way. She doesn't dislike him. She wants to like him more. But right now she knows that another hour of conversation on the meaning of the symbols in Revelation will end up totally one-sided.

" . . . and so the writers of the various books, you see, were not dictated to by God — "

"Would you like a hamburger?" she suddenly blurts out, and she is sorry immediately, because it sounds so irreverent.

Silence. He seems dumbstruck. She slaps at a mosquito on her arm. She knows she has blown it. Hamburgers, of course, have no place in canonicity. He says nothing for a long time, and only the hum of mosquitoes is there with them. Finally he eases up on the brake and clutch, his hands slide off the wheel in tired motions, and he turns the key. *Blessed music of a four-cylinder Volkswagen!*

"Of course," he says shortly, a bit miffed, even a little hurt? They say nothing as he drives to McDonald's. He gets two hamburgers. They eat, not saying much. It is their first and last meal together, she knows that for certain. She tries to patch it up by opening the conversation about school, her classes; then, deliberately to get him into other interests, she asks, "What do you have in mind for the future?" But he is still mulling over his unfinished treatise on the canon, of which the half-eaten hamburger in his hands is a kind of symbol. He doesn't know about his future, he says politely. "That is God's to reveal in time." Of course, Midge realizes, what else could he say? Conversation is gone again, and the smell of onions is coming on strong.

"I think I'll be late," she says. He cranks up the VW, still munching half-heartedly on his burger, and drives her back to the campus. Midge R. will taste onions all night trying to get to sleep. It was not a very good date — not at all.

"I don't know which one is worse," she says, commenting on her years of trying to find a Christian man who fits her own image of a "balanced" male, "that theologian who didn't know what to do with his hands or the wolf man who has his hands all over me."

Midge typifies a good many Christian young women who from the beginning of their dating years have accumulated or are accumulating a rather miserable track record of trying to figure out single men or connect with one for life. "Maybe it's the same for the non-Christian too," Midge admits. "But I think we have more acute extremes in Christian culture for some reason. On one end is the guy who feels a date is like running through a ring of fire and is doing all he can not to get burnt. On the other is the guy who is a ball of fire and wants me to share the heat. Is there no middle ground?"

Of course, Midge does admit that "now and then I at least found a date who didn't fall apart if his hand happened to brush mine as we walked, and there were some who came close to showing some balance." Nevertheless, she adds, "There is still far too much tension between Christian men and women. There is an inability to relax, a pressure that seems to stem from their uncertainty of what is right to do, with or for each other. There is too much sexual tension, too much jitteriness about it being there, and then of course too much display of it by the guy who has already decided he might as well do what comes naturally. Sometimes I wonder how any Christians finally get married . . . to me, it has been that bad."

Well, what Midge did not see in those two extremes — the theological scholar with his hands frozen on the wheel and the "wolf man" with his hands all over her — is that both were practicing a certain kind of "ego mastery." All men are driven by it in some form when it comes to their relationship with women. The ultimate and the ugliest form of ego mastery is rape, where the man's mind drives his emotions crazy so that he forces himself on a woman.

The date who used his theological knowledge to demonstrate his spiritual powers as ego mastery over Midge failed in his attempt to impress her. He wound up being a bore. It was not entirely the subject, but the academic approach to it. He is that "straight type" who feels that a Christian date with a Christian girl should be "Christian" — and that means the conversation should be Christian. Midge doesn't mind Christian subjects; she welcomes discussion on any or all of them. But those esoteric areas of canonicity and symbolic forms in Revelation are not always appropriate for a date or for provoking a two-way exchange. At any rate, though, this man was trying to make his "manly" impression in the only way he knew. Perhaps the girl he is looking for is someone who will sit at his feet in starry-eyed wonder at his ability to expound on biblical and theological truth. Some day he may find such a girl. But he is not for Midge, and she knows it. He needs balance, as Midge insists.

In the meantime, he is not comfortable with the closeness of that VW cab. Yet he would probably be uncomfortable out of it too, because that would mean he wouldn't know what to do with his hands. In his careful, almost too precise pose behind the wheel, he is conscious of his own sexuality that a girl arouses in him. That too is part of his male drive. No man can fully deny that it is there, no matter how theologically lofty his conversation and no matter how precise he is in not allowing any signal system that might be construed by her as the beginning of a "pass." No matter how he views Midge as "neutral friendship," he will feel the pressure of that sexuality. It is not abnormal. It is a healthy sign of his manhood. What is abnormal is his inability to relax with it. If he turns out to be a bore, it is only because he is afraid of "intimacy." Intimacy connotes sexual touch, and that, he fears, will characterize him to her in ways he does not want to convey. He hopes his mastery will come through more in terms of his scholarship — but few women want a cold scholar on a four-hour date.

The other type of man, the "ball of fire" type, as Midge calls him, is seeking to demonstrate his ego mastery through sex. For him, a man is a sexual being, and a woman is a sexual being, so "who needs talk?" He may be driven that way because of a number of factors in his childhood or in his training. If he has not had enough manly images around him as a child or in early adolescence, he will either assume a more feminine outlook or he will become aggressive sexually to make up for it. Midge does not realize that many a young Christian man, surrounded most of his life by the *spiritual* definitions of manhood — that do not allow for the chemistry of physical manhood — will sometimes try to compensate by proving himself sexually. Often a husband will try to find ratification for himself as a man in his mastery of his wife in the same way. As a result, she complains that he is "wanting sex all the time."

Ego mastery is a strong compulsion in a man in relationship to a woman. It is something mysteriously deep within his glands, an explosive force affecting mind and emotion. The need to command, to perform, to take the lead, to show strength is in the nature of manhood. Much of what a man feels he needs to do to gain that mastery — as if the woman will think less of him if he does not — is grounded in myth. But it is there nevertheless, ever since Stone Age man clubbed the woman of his choice and dragged her off to his cave. Spiritual values have enabled a man to control that mastery, hopefully within the boundaries of spiritual character, but it still comes out in various forms, and sometimes not always as expected. So the bland, boring type who talks to get mastery and verify himself as man by his intellectual powers and the man whom Midge says she "has to keep fighting off all the time" are both driven by the same mysterious manly ego. Both are seeking to make a masterful impression on her.

For Midge to judge them as "hopeless extremes" is true to a point; but it is important for her to know why they are that way before she enters into marriage with Doug. Because even he may have certain egocentricities that may not show up until six months after the honeymoon. She ought to be prepared for that.

Further, the extremes represented in these two types of men

do not mean that one is more manly than the other or that one is more Christian. Both have the capacities to be men in the fullest sense, men who make good husbands. Because one keeps his hands in front of him and talks theology while the other is all over her in sexual aggression does not put one or the other in a lesser light as a man. As to the Christian judgment of them, the same is true. It may be true that the sexual aggressor does not understand that Midge is not "on the make" simply because she accepts him as a date; but to conclude that he is a "runaway express train driven by the expanded pressure of his sex" and therefore without character is to misjudge him. In the same light, to judge the theological scholar, who seems nervous about his own sexuality and is leaning on his intellect to impress her, as "retarded in both his physical and spiritual life" is also a misjudgment.

However, Midge poses a legitimate question. There must and should be some middle ground. There ought to be what could be called an "intimate friendship" relationship that both Christian men and women could cultivate and appreciate without the tensions of sexuality forcing false behavior and then false judgments.

"Intimacy," however, frightens both men and women within church culture. It connotes sexual demand and sexual surrender. Friendship must be kept within the boundaries of a "Hi!" when they meet, a brief but polite conversation, maybe a few laughs over a Coke. That is about the extent of the intimacy the church or its institutions will allow.

Midge put it this way: "Some guys I like to be around, and it has nothing really to do with sex, though I may be attracted to them in some measure by sex. We are fearfully and wonderfully made this way, after all. But I want to be with them, not for the sexual chemistry, but because they are people who encourage me, who relax me, who have such wide dimensions in their personalities and spiritual intellects that I honestly learn from them. I learn more from them than I do on dates with a guy trapped in a VW cab because the sexual tension is not there. I like such a friendship where that man can put his arm around my shoulders in affection and not have to worry about my reaction nor do I have to feel that I am compromising something sexually in that touch."

Andrew Greeley, the popular Catholic columnist, in his book *Sexual Intimacy*, defined this kind of friendship:

I define friendship as an intimate relationship between two human beings in which both become sufficiently open to one another that they are able, at least to some extent, to put aside their fears and suspicions and enjoy the pains and pleasures of vulnerability. Living with friendship and living with sexuality is essentially the art of living with our capacity for intimacy, with both the demands intimacy makes and the rewards it gives.[1]

Christianity does not yet provide this middle ground between the sexes. Consequently, single men are afraid of dating single women because the relationship "could get complicated" or "the girl might presume too much." Single women likewise are in fear of the men they date, because they are not sure just how much they have to compromise sexually in order to keep his good will and to be asked out again.

As Midge says, "The single girl who doesn't have many dates is afraid to deny a sexual aggressor for fear he won't ask to date her again and will pass the word around that she is a 'toad' — meaning she won't give. A girl is caught then between giving in and being asked again, or holding off and being labeled a prude. Too many girls have given in, and what happens then is that she gets a bad reputation. This happens as much among Christian men and women as among non-Christians. Men have a way of passing that around the locker rooms, and nothing is more demolishing for a girl than to find out she's labeled that way."

Men suffer the same form of fracture, however, despite what women think. They are never sure how they are to demonstrate their ego mastery in terms of what the woman expects. Some men are free and easy and relate to women in that balanced way that Midge looks for. Other men are caught between the spiritual disciplines and the need to be more intimate. To make the wrong move is to label him either a "bore" or a "naked ape," to use familiar campus terminology.

In order to avoid these tensions and possibly the loss of self-image, the young need to build intimate friendships that do not force sexual compromise or pose confusion about how to conduct a relationship. This is an excellent beginning place to develop healthier and more permanent future marriages. If a single man and woman learn to cultivate intimate friendships — that is, to draw from each other the strengths and encouragements each has to give without any bartering on the sexual level — they will be able to discern later between true love and sexual fascination.

But for a man or a woman to enter into close, intimate friendships like this — sharing with each other and not being afraid to show affection even by touch — means taking risks. It also means a willingness to become vulnerable.

Andrew Greeley put it this way:

> One experiences vulnerability in such friendships because if one reaches out and the other doesn't respond, what then? What if one exposes one's need and is rejected? There is perhaps more risk in taking than in being taken because the taking partner plays the more active role and looks more foolish and ridiculous when he is rejected. The fear of appearing ridiculous is one of the most powerful obstacles to human intimacy.
>
> Because we lack the courage to take risks, the courage to give ourselves and to accept the gift of another we are therefore unable to take advantage of anything more than a tiny fraction of the joys, physical and psychological, that God has intended us to have in this world.
>
> There are times when we are complete mysteries to each other, and there are times when we seem obvious and transparent . . . but we need help from the other if we are to reveal ourselves both because we need his assurance that self-revelation is safe and because it is a delight to have him share the act by which we reveal ourselves.[2]

This experience of intimate friendship is what is missing from many marriages too. For while there is sexual exchange in marriage, and this is the culmination of what has been friendship previous to the marriage, the lack of continuing intimacy outside of sex causes the misunderstandings that can fragment the relationship. "Once a man gets what he wants out of marriage, meaning sex, he is not as much interested in the needs of a woman in other areas," one frustrated wife confessed. "He loses his courteousness, his protectiveness, his sense of primal value of me that we had in courtship. I find myself becoming then primarily a sex partner to assuage his urges and not much more. Sex holds us shakily together, but for how long?"

A man, however, is not concerned only with sex and the satisfaction of his sexual needs in marriage. His problem is that he has not

had opportunity enough to experience intimate friendships with
members of the opposite sex earlier in his life so that he could learn
what the values of a woman are to him besides sex. And it works both
ways. While Christian single girls are fighting men off and while
men are fighting to dominate, they inevitably develop a distrust of
intersexual relationships. This distrust will drive some women to a
lifetime of celibacy or a sexual immaturity about marriage. It will
drive some men to non-Christian women where affairs with single
women are not so complicated by internal pressures of what is right
or wrong.

But as Greeley puts it,

> Friendship is a rhythm of conquest and surrender. In a healthy
> friendship we never completely conquer the other nor do we
> have complete surrender. . . . Intimacy is nevertheless painful.
> We must be confident of our own attractiveness to offer our-
> selves. . . . There are powerful fears in our personalities that say
> that being conquered and conquering is not worth the effort.[3]

He goes on pointedly to nail the issue where it belongs.

> What light does the Christian symbol system throw on the
> anxieties, the fears, the ambiguities, involved in human inti-
> macy? The real ambiguity is rooted in man's pathetic desire for
> unity with others and his abiding fear of unity, of his passionate
> delight in his own vulnerability combined with his terror of
> being vulnerable, in his profound enjoyment of the sweetness
> of being able to trust and his bitter responses to the possibility
> of having his trust betrayed.
>   In other words, man desperately wants friendship and love
> (despite women who say all they want is sex), but he is terribly
> afraid of taking the traumatic risk of self-exposure [such as the
> theological scholar who kept on talking theology, perhaps in
> fear of that exposure] that is necessary for love. Shame, a
> conviction of his own worthlessness and unlovability tells man
> that the risk is not worth taking and that even if he should take
> it, he would be betrayed.[4]

So the theologian uses his intellect and theology as a means to
impress but at the same time hide behind when he's with Midge or
any girl. The sexual aggressor tries to take the shortcuts and get from
sex what he does not know how to give in terms of his true self, his
inner needs, his own sense of uncertainty about himself.

A woman needs to know that Christian man goes through these

conflicts with single women as much as she does with single men. That early childhood training, loyalty to pledges of the institution, fear of violating purity — or worse yet, being rejected — are all battles that have to be fought as he seeks identity with himself and the opposite sex. Midge, then, needs to be willing to experience a date with a man that winds up as failure with only the smell of onions to testify to that failure. Knowing why it failed, or perhaps knowing some of these tensions in a man, she might be able to avoid future failure and the pain of a misspent evening. A woman may have to risk the sexual aggressor in her desire for nothing more than an intimate friendship, provided she has some sense of knowing why he is trying to get from sex what he thinks he can't get in any other way. That may not be a highly successful evening either, but in the knowing there is at least some area in which the single girl can make her appeal to him. Both men want to avoid the stigma of being a "bore" or a "naked ape." Their Christianity is a standard they live by too, and they desire to make it work just as much as the woman.

This developing of wholesome, intimate friendships that do not force sexual compromise or presume it demands an openness and a willingness of both sexes to cultivate it. The fear of what intimacy must lead to must be turned aside. A man must learn to put aside his sexual drive as a means of self-gratification and see in that woman an individual who is more than an object for conquest. The woman, in turn, must accept friendship from a man as a challenge to her to give back what she senses he really needs from her which is not sexual. If the body of Christ cannot create the milieu in which such wholesome relationships can develop without a great deal of worry and fret, there will always remain those uneasy tensions which will be carried into marriage.

If Christianity promises anything at all it is that quality of trust that says the individual is more than a composite of sexual pressures and, therefore, those who own Christ can be trusted to protect each other in the totality of their persons. Men who have had a history of a Christian culture that persistently surrounded them with an aura of suspicion about their intersexual activities are men who find it difficult to relate honestly with a woman in a true sense of intimacy. Men who have never been trusted as boys find sexual encounter a demoralizing experience, because they have never been taught how to relate to the opposite sex when alone with them. The story of the man who invited his mother to go with him and his wife on their honeymoon is not so far-fetched after all, and though some people view this with amusement, it is actually a symbol of the tragedy that hangs over too many Christian young men in their sexual experiences.

The church institutions that see the importance of this will have to reckon with the fact that when two people do cultivate intimate friendships with each other, they must be allowed some demonstration of their sexual attractiveness. There may be a kiss, an embrace, even a caress . . . but to conclude that such gestures must constitute a violation of the sexual mores of Christendom is to deny the trust two people have in each other — a trust the Holy Spirit gives. If distrust prevails, this will only create more distrust of each other, and ultimately marriage will be entered into far too hastily just to get reprieve from the tensions. This is a shaky base upon which to establish a lifetime union.

Concerning those who won't allow this to occur, Greeley says:

> There is a great deal of cynical leering about such relationships among the unsophisticated whose notions of sexuality never get beyond the locker room humor and among the highly sophisticated, who might think that this 'swinging' is a healthy form of sexual outlet and that incomplete relationships are frustrating and unhealthy.[5]

Midge did, gratefully, experience such an intimate friendship for one year at college. "He was an artist, one class ahead of me. We just struck it off together from the start. He helped me in my math; I helped him in his literature class. But we were drawn to each other, not on sexual chemistry so much as on the openness and trust we had with each other. I wouldn't say it was brotherly, but it was platonic really. We talked about our lives, about our problems. I cried with him when he lost out in the art show in Chicago. He cried with me when I got a D in math one quarter. Sometimes he would move up beside me when I was walking across campus and put his arm around my shoulder, as if he knew I was down. He had a great grasp of practical spirituality, and I always knew he could lift me just by the way he explained how God fit into it all. I could be with Rod any time of the day or night for that matter and be perfectly safe with him, even secure. People watching would think we had something really going between us; but both of us knew that it wasn't that at all. It wasn't love, the kind that led to marriage; it was the love that I really felt Christ had in mind for His own. I had no shame in embracing Rod in public, for his strength and encouragement to me. If there was sexuality between us, neither of us felt it crowding up into what we had. When he graduated and left school, I had lost a friend who was everything a woman could ask for as she tries to grow up. I cried a lot when he left, but after a while I took the time to thank God I had him for the time I did, for what I had learned from him, from being so close to a man and yet not having to have that sexual tension interfering with the beauty of that friendship.

"My dating totaled out to be mostly disappointment until Rod came along. Up to then my attempt to display affection with a man I liked but who was uptight about intimacy was like a green garter snake trying to make love to a garden hose — there is similarity in contour and color but that's as far as it goes. Or else it was a test of my gymnastic ability to get a hammerlock on him before he could get one on me. I yearned for someone, some man, with whom I could find that neutral ground where we could share, laugh, cry, and learn from each other, as I did with Rod. I wasn't looking for platonic relationships with every date; all I wanted was some opportunity to know the man and have him know me in hopes that we might hit it off, and that God would have some opportunity to show me if this was the man for my life or not. . . ." Midge suffered far too long in disappointing experiences with a variety of men.

Most men and women do suffer this way because the church has taken the stand that to allow two people of the opposite sex to experience "intimacy" before marriage, even in the way Midge and Rod did, is to invite the ultimate calamity of sexual compromise. And that is why Christian women go on, patiently or not so patiently, indulging the terrified scholars who are afraid of their own vulnerability or fighting off the male infants who insist that sex is all that men and women are about.

More important, if there is no attempt to build or encourage friendships that are intimate, then it seems almost inevitable that many Christian marriages will run a staggered course. Emotional maturity is essential to make a union work, and it must be there prior to the union, not left to be developed — hopefully — with the years. The rhythm of giving and receiving in intersexual roles between man and woman, having been learned early in life in an atmosphere of trust, is the key to disarming tensions and mending the fractures that could occur later in marriage.

Otherwise, the only alternative left for the Christian man-woman union that suffers from immaturity and tension is the one that suggests the traditional authoritarian line of the male who must have sexual dominance in order to be kept happy. This reduces the woman to nothing more than a temptress whose success with her man is determined on the basis of how well she can seduce him and even coddle him.

In an article in *McCall's* magazine, Barbara Grizzuti Harrison did a study on two women authors, Marabel Morgan and Helen Andelin, the front runners in the crusade to maintain the submissive role of women and the sexual dominance of men. Harrison says that Andelin, in her book *Fascinating Womanhood*, implores

> a yielding to her husband's rule, opinions, discretion or judg-ments . . . a wife must welcome tedious dialogue . . . whether she agrees with him or not does not matter. So she sits there and admires, not his words, not his ideas, but his manliness . . . when a woman surrenders . . . relinquishing what may appear to be rights, she gains every advantage . . . a husband will do anything within his power to make her happy . . . men never want women to grow up completely.[6]

This is not only an insult to a man, but is a gross and dangerous miscalculation of what he wants in a woman. To allow it to stand is to demean the woman; instead of an intelligent being, she is a conniv-ing, wily, beguiling Delilah. There is no communication involved; there is only a childish pandering that feeds the myth of what man is and desires in a wife and breeds an unhealthy male dominance that does not bring equal fulfillment. There is no intimacy in that rela-tionship and there is no true friendship. There is no sharing. There is no value other than the thing called "manliness" or "womanhood." There is nothing there but the raw, exposed politics of sexual diplomacy.

There is no beauty emerging in this view of a wife's role with her husband. And without beauty, there is only boredom for the man who does not want a doting woman subject to his every whim, but a total person who can complement him, discuss with him, opinionate with him, and intelligently exchange with him.

"Dispense with any air of strength and ability," Andelin goes on in her advice to women, "and acquire instead an air of frail dependency. And while you're at it, be sure your voice has a 'cooing effect' or 'purring quality'; practice 'baby talk.' "[7]

This is simply seeing a man as a sexual plaything to be appeased, to be manipulated — it is to give something in order to get something in return. It is a sign of a frightened woman, a woman who is insecure and totally uncertain of herself or her man.

Harrison went on to quote Andelin, who states, "In his pleasure at having himself admired, the man seldom notices that his conversation is not understood."[8]

Harrison comments on this point by saying, "I could not find one man who did not regard that kind of duplicity and obsequiousness as an insult; one male friend said, 'If I want a dumb receptacle for my conversation and confidences, I'll talk to my cat.' "[9]

Andelin adds that "if a man does not love his wife heart and soul, it is the wife's fault . . . when women correct their own mistakes they can bring about a wonderful loving response in a man . . . independent of any direct effort on the part of their husbands."[10]

Harrison comments on this by saying, "To regard men in that light it seems to me is to regard them as moles. I read contempt for men (as well as ambivalence and confusion) in the declaration that 'he has a right to himself, to be weak, lazy, to neglect his duty or even to fail. This is his department.' I see contempt for men in that statement 'a man always considers a woman to be better than he and would be disappointed to see her fall from her level to his.' "[11]

Of course, both Andelin and Morgan have said things that have helped women in their relationship with men, but these specific statements fall far short of what a man truly is and what he looks for in his wife. Intimate friendship is something that negates this false presumption and, therefore, it is all the more necessary to cultivate before marriage so that marriage becomes truly *intimate* and not simply sexual.

Jesus Himself was not afraid to cultivate that kind of friendship with Martha and Mary. There was nothing sexual about it, but as a man He drew something from that friendship with the opposite sex that was positive and rewarding, even as the women did from Him. Though marriage was not in the plan for Him, He demonstrated His human manliness in desiring the company of women and cultivating an intimacy that was beautiful and poignant in the few occasions that the Bible records. Both women respected Him as a man but did not seek special favor from Him by some form of sexual manipulation. They could feel comfortable with His masculinity and He with their femininity, and by the intimacy they cultivated together there grew a bond of friendship and love that presumed nothing in terms of sex.

Parents who witness this kind of relationship between their daughter and a man, or vice versa, are suspicious of it and after awhile will say, "Look, if that thing you have with him (or her) is not going anywhere, forget it!"

They are afraid of "that thing," afraid it will lead to sexual calamity. But "that thing" is something which could very well complement both of them — not something sexual, but something deep, something sensitive, something that is true friendship and that is building in them a maturity about genuine intersexual roles. They may never marry each other, but what they learn from each other will go a long way toward preparing them for a successful union with that person with whom they will truly fall in love.

This intimate friendship can give a woman a view of a man that she can never have in any other way, and vice versa. If this does not occur and the other shallow, even false conclusions about what men look for in a woman remain, then marriages will indeed become, as Shakespeare said in *Romeo and Juliet*, "straining harsh chords and unpleasing sharps."

But Midge R. did find her man. She waited until she was twenty-nine to find him, a special benefit of that "middle ground" of intimate friendships.

"The day he stopped to change a flat on my car in the parking lot, there was something in him I felt very strongly attracted to," she recalls. "When he asked me out on our first date, I sensed a rapport immediately, and I thought this would be something beautiful like I had with Rod. But with Doug we moved beyond what that relationship was; we began to grow toward each other more. I began to sense the difference now between what was platonic with Rod and what I was feeling with Doug. I sensed a powerful attractiveness to him sexually, in my total emotions. Because I knew there was a difference in chemistry, I knew that here was something I had to be protective about, to guard closely, not to be flip about. The months that passed were a continual growth in our relationship that was

God's unmistakable leading for me . . . this was it. And I knew he felt the same."

For Midge there was no need to trade off her sex and his needs for favor or acceptance. Her patience to wait for the right man, rather than giving in to panic about not finding him, brought her the rich reward. Perhaps that experience with Rod, that bridge of "intimate friendship," kept her from seeing the man-woman relationship as mainly sexual and thus saved her from compromising simply to gain the favor of a man. Too many single Christian women have been that route, and they have the emotional scars to prove it. No one can tell what "bridge-building experiences of intimacy" actually do for either a man or a woman in preparing them for the real thing. In Midge's case, she sensed the value of it in that it helped her to know the difference in the true love relationship.

And yet in her year of dating Doug, Midge had to prove some things of critical importance to both of them. As powerfully attracted as they were to each other, they had to ask the big question sooner or later if it was to be a relationship of permanence. Some take the answer for granted. Midge and Doug did not. Some are afraid to ask it. Midge was too, but she finally did. She had to risk that big moment to prove finally that what they had together was not simply "chemistry" but something much more enduring.

4.

OF LOVE

AND SEX

He is the half part of a blessed man,
Left to be finished by such as she;
And she a fair divided excellence,
Whose fullness of perfection lies in him.

— Shakespeare

"It's been a year . . . do you think it's time?" he said, holding her close.

"When is it ever time?" she asked, content to be right where she was, to let time go on and be judged by someone else.

"It has something to do with love, I guess," he said lightly.

"When is it love then?"

"I . . . don't know. Aren't two people supposed to know?"

"My grandmother always told me God would let me know."

"Well?"

"How does He let me know?"

Silence. "You have peace about it, right?"

"I get stormy times too . . . about you."

"Bad storms? Uncertainties?"

"No, silly . . . my emotions go into turmoil when I think about you, when I'm away from you."

"Isn't that something God-given then?"

"How do I know it isn't just sexual fascination with you?"

"That's part of it . . . it has to be."

"But it's not the same as love, is it?" she asked, looking up into his face, a strong face with reflections there that showed the generous gifts of compassion, laughter, and life along with a meditative tone that said he knew God and loved Him. In those blue eyes that could hide nothing of his character was a man of stature, of sensitivity, a man who could stand firm in life, receive it, give it, and hold it in his grasp. How could she not love a man like this, who was neither a tense, timid man, afraid of her and her sex nor an insistent, pawing, demanding conqueror who tried to use her for his own sense of ego mastery? Yet she took the time for caution, when everything in her rebelled at doing so. Ring or no ring, she wanted to be sure.

No, sexual attraction and love are not the same. She had asked the right question. "No," he said to her, "it isn't . . . but we have some things going for us that we know are right — "

"But you don't like abstract art — "

"And you don't like the smell of sulfuric acid or chemistry labs."

"And I hate Chinese food . . . you gorge yourself on it — "

"Your rib-eye steaks and pizza would give me the gout in a month — "

"You like Johnny Cash and that John Denver," she went on. "I can't get excited about either . . . they will never come up to Brahms or Sibelius or Wagner."

"I might go along with that," he admitted. "But you like the Gospels where I like Proverbs and the Psalms."

"So what do we have going for us now besides the sexual?" she asked, almost holding her breath, terrified of the answer the question begged, an answer she did not want to get for fear it would force the issue.

"Knowing all that," he went on, his breath warm on her forehead, "can you walk away from me now. Can I walk away from you? Are those things all that important? What holds us together — what has held us together for a year?"

It couldn't be platonic, she knew. Not like the relationship she had had with Rod. What was the difference? The powerful sexual attraction? Even now as he held her, she felt the strength of his arms, the warmth of his body; there was that sexual stirring within her again, the rising to him in the strange and mysterious drive of the God-given chemistry that had shaped nations, destroyed kingdoms, and brought ruin or ecstasy to millions from the beginning of time.

But was it love? Or was it sex? After a year of laughing together, sharing together, touching, holding, probing deeply into each other's lives for the meanings there and for God's wisdom and purpose for them, could it be otherwise? And yet she hesitated. Was the ideal image still driving the wedge between them? The perfect match? They were not perfectly matched. He was a chemist, she an artist; their likes in food, music, and recreation were different. They had one thing that held fast and was common to them — their commitment to Christ and His will for them in life. This they had, and perhaps it was this which mattered the most. Without it, they had nothing to guarantee their years ahead. But did not others have this commitment too? Was it the one factor that made the final difference?

It was right for Midge to ask those questions. Every woman should. Midge should wonder if Doug is pushing aside the differences under the pressure of his need for sexual oneness with her, his need now after a year to complete this union for fulfillment in that area alone. These are two people caught in a sexually free society — a time of coed dorms, a time when campus life is free sex with no other thought of human values beyond that. Were they, then, simply coming to some kind of impasse in the sexual area — the strong need for each other's bodies that would drive them to ignore the elements of intrinsic value that had to be there if they were to live their years together in happiness?

But in the asking, if it becomes too much asking, Midge could lose him with that "sense of ideal." Many single women (and men) spend too much time with "check lists" of things that must be there in a man before she consents to think of marriage. The fantasies of childhood and adolescence can become adult expectations of that "perfect match" when there really isn't such a thing.

In fact, the total plus factors of two people do not really provide the arc of power between them. It takes the plus-minus factors on both sides, each knowing there are strengths and weaknesses in the other that are to complement each other. This brings that all-important mutual dependence and respect that spins off that great word called love. Doug had his weaknesses and strengths; she had hers. Doug had his tastes in things; she had hers. If it were not so, their lives would run the same courses, but the explorations into other domains would not be there. In other words, opposites do attract, and these opposites are not detractors in the marriage union — at least not in the terms described above — but often they are the necessary dimensions two people can give each other to bring excitement and freshness to their lives.

The woman who looks for the ideal man — the embodiment of her fantasy life who has all the talent, personality, character, aggressiveness, popularity *that she does not have*, a man who will bring the dull star of her own life to new brilliance — is making a serious mistake. That lopsided kind of marriage, where all she has to give such a powerhouse is her sex, is going to leave her high and dry in the end as he becomes bored with her inability to contribute anything to his life already loaded with strengths. There has to be that reasonable complementary level of exchange — strength for his weakness, and vice versa.

Love, in any case, is not based on the totality of the exact likenesses or the exact strengths or weaknesses each has, or even tastes for that matter. Love is there in Doug's one pointed question: "Knowing all that — what differences in tastes we may have — can we walk away from each other?" If either one of them can and feels no pull, then love probably does not reign there. There has been a convenient relationship perhaps, even an intimate friendship such as Midge had with Rod; there may have been a powerful sexual attraction, but it will not solve that big question when the issues become larger, when each comes to know the other too well in marriage.

For a man who cannot walk away from this girl, above all other girls, it means there is a *physical chemistry* that cannot be ignored. Call it a composite of sexual attraction on the one hand; but call it also a powerful drawing to this girl whose *personality* and *character* and very *being* are mysteriously *his*. It's what makes him eat too much or not at all; it's what preoccupies him in every unoccupied moment of his day. It either makes him act like a zombie or climb brick walls hand over hand. It's enough to make an ape out of a gentleman and a gentleman out of an ape. Men throughout the centuries have tried to explain it — no one has done so yet. A man *knows;* that's the long and short of it. He knows the *chemical* thing is there, that the mixture is right, heady, too powerful to ignore. Man starts there, with the chemistry. He is made that way. And once a man is struck by this God-given pull, he will not be easily pushed aside. Sometimes this chemistry can keep two people together when all else fails.

But what Doug is also stating in that one question, that one test is that beyond the physical chemistry is a desire to *commit* to her for life. For when a man is convinced that this is the girl, *she is all he wants.* Not just for the moment, not just until the sexual pressure is eased, but he wants this girl to be with him — permanently. Commitment is something a man does not give to many people. But when he senses the right mate for him, he is fully prepared to put his life on the line for her. As melodramatic as that sounds, women need to know the fallacy of the notion they entertain too often that "man plays the field" and is at best "fickle." They do not realize how possessive a man becomes when he commits himself to a woman. He is willing to risk his own vulnerability, to risk rejection, to risk the responsibility of union with one person. Once he faces the big question — "Can I walk away from her and be happy the rest of my life?" — and knows he cannot, he is ready to give that girl all of himself in the totality of his strength, his mind, his will. And Midge must do the same. Chemistry is one thing; commitment is another. Especially when the chemistry begins to wear off some years later.

Commitment does mean "for better or worse," and the man has no questions about it, even if there are times when it will be "worse." It is a commitment to give that girl all he can in the *value* of her as *a person,* as she is to him, certainly as she is to God. What Doug is asking Midge is that she face that question, as he has faced it and answered it. Midge must feel the same, or there can be no union, for there is no sure ground upon which marriage can rest unless love works both ways.

For a man there is the urge for *completeness* from this commitment. Man is at best a lonely being until he has found his partner, the one person who can complete his life. He is lonely in the spatial sense, and he is lonely in the spiritual sense. A Christian man like Doug knows love in terms of the mysterious God-given bond he feels with that girl. This is not true of all intersexual relationships. It is not enough to feel love in terms of a completion physically, even emotionally; a Christian man seeks totality for himself in a union with a *spiritual* being. It does not mean a perfect understanding of all that is spiritual. Midge may never know much about canonicity or the whole overview of theology. What Doug looks for in her is a value she holds as being in Christ, in His Spirit. Doug wants completion in the Godhead as it were, and the girl he loves will share that spiritual being as he shares it. It is not a question of knowledge; it is a question of spiritual sensitivity. The spiritual is too often put aside as the lesser part of a man's love, because women think he is more concerned with the physical, the mental, the emotional. But any man who knows Christ also knows he can never be complete until the girl he marries rises to his need for *spiritual* companionship. There are no tests to be taken on the sixty-six books of the Bible, no marathon Bible memory contests. It is simply that a man reaches out for that common ground upon which he can relate his deeper feelings about God with her, as she with him.

What Shakespeare said, then, is not true, though it does too often happen:

> No sooner met but they looked; no sooner looked but they loved; no sooner loved but they sighed; no sooner sighed but they asked one another the reason; no sooner knew the reason but they sought the remedy.

That is obviously an oversimplification. A man is not simply looking for a "remedy," although it may be true that there are "looks," "sighs," and "the reason" which form the basis for honest searching about a relationship. But it is not true that only the woman does the searching for cause while the man does the pressuring for a quick "remedy."

Midge, of course, has sense enough to know that a man's sexual powers can and do lead him to ignore the differences that may prohibit forging a union. His mind is fixed on one predominant point at times: "I want this woman's body, and I can't think of anything more sublime than fifty years of possessing it for myself in all the ecstasies and sheer pleasure it now holds for me." A man will risk the differences he may have with that woman, he will risk the minus factors; he even will accede to whatever the woman says she needs in a man to have that woman for himself. Case upon case of men, not Christian, who have consented to become Christians, when the woman has insisted on that for marriage, have shown this to be true. The aftermath of calamity then is all too evident.

But at any rate, here is a man willing to explore the big question with Midge and to be honest about that question and many more. Yet in knowing there are those small differences in taste between them, he insists that their love rests on that one critical point: their inability to break from each other and their deeply felt desire to become one. And the man will press the point until there is a decision one way or the other.

Love really can be tested finally on no other point, and it dare not be tested on anything less. A man and a woman may have all the perfectly matched tastes in a thousand and one things; they may say they are "ideal for each other" based on those likenesses. But until they agree to spend the next forty years together and realize they want it with no one else, they have not loved. Enjoying some of the same things, having likes and similarities in taste, is certainly important, of course; total opposites can be as short-circuiting to a relationship as the total match is nondynamic. Balance is critical. But Doug is right: what differences they have about food, art, or literature are not the final test, because each can learn to appreciate these from the other.

No, it still comes down to that big question of Doug's. It must be faced. The answer is critical in terms of whether they will both be able to survive the years of storm and tumult ahead, the tensions, the imbalances, even the testy exchanges. To know from the beginning that life is impossible without the other is to know a *fusion* that will not be easily broken. This fusion goes beyond the mere surface charge of sexual attractiveness or any other emotional chemistry that passes for love.

There is a cost in accepting a relationship that is *fused*, where two people are literally welding themselves to each other for a lifetime in the totality of their beings. The same test came through in Jesus' response to the rich young ruler in Mark 10:17-22. When the young man, perhaps in the great emotion of the moment, asked what he should do to inherit eternal life, he was posing a question similar to Midge's, "What is love?" The Lord sifted him out in his eagerness to be bound up in the apparent "glamour" of the kingdom of God by the statement that begged the question: "Then Jesus beholding him loved him, and said unto him, One thing thou lackest: go thy way, sell whatsoever thou hast, and give to the poor, and thou shalt have treasure in heaven: and come, take up the cross, and follow me" (v. 21).

The young man, undoubtedly a bit shook by the answer, concluded that the price was too high. "And he was sad at that saying, and went away grieved: for he had great possessions" (v. 22).

One thing lacking. A willingness to be fused? No. But a fusion at the expense of what he considered more important became the issue. So a young man's hero worship — even love, if so strong a term can be used — came under the heat of the big test. What was a case of spiritual union with Christ can be compared with two people considering marital union. One must be willing to abandon some part of himself or herself in order to effect that necessary fusion. For the young man in question, it was too much to ask. Better then that he was forced to face the question than become disloyal under the pressure later on. Whatever he had in mind with his eagerness to be a part of Christ and His kingdom, no matter how lofty his intent, no matter how strong his desire for that fusion, he failed to grasp the full implications of what he was asking. Jesus was faithful in posing the demands, and Doug was faithful to Midge in the same way.

"Knowing all that (the differences we may have), can you walk away from me now?" is a tremendously loaded question and rightly so. Like the rich young ruler, if it cannot be answered properly in terms of "no, I cannot walk away from you," then a man feels uneasy. A woman should too. But too often a woman will hedge on the question, mostly because she is not prepared for it; she has come to presume from the mythical measurements of a man that he has only one test: sexual compatability. As important as that may be, and as difficult as it is for a man not to make that the basis of love, he does seek something deeper, much deeper.

The woman, surrounded as she is with the cultural images that say a man equates love with sex, cannot believe or even accept the fact that he has other criteria for a permanent relationship. She has come to believe that her sex alone looks for "character and values beyond the sexual," while the man is so made that he can only gauge a relationship on the physical level.

At any rate, Midge now stands at the line where other women have, faced with a question loaded with implications. It is baffling in a sense because it has nothing to do with sex per se. The danger is that the woman will push it aside and resort to what she *thinks* he means — a sexual test. If she interprets it that way, unwilling or unable to see anything else in the question, she will have failed him — and will in all probability lose him.

The question then is: can this *courtship* be saved?

5.

MAN'S LOVE —
CONFLICT AND
CONTRADICTION

Alas! that love, so gentle in his view,
  should be so tyrannous and rough
    in proof.

— Shakespeare

Will the premarital sex test spoil Rock Hunter? And, likewise, will it spoil the one to whom he has declared his love? The film years back called "Will Success Spoil Rock Hunter?" illustrated that it can. What was a measure of success in that film can be carried over to what a man feels he has accomplished in sexual conquest.

The modern sexologist would disagree, taking the position that intercourse with the woman to whom a man has committed himself is not wrong. In their view, a wedding ceremony is but a poor ritualistic ratification to proceed. The world's changing values on sex would support the view, and a "situational ethic" would espouse that what is the highest good for the other and therefore the epitome of love in that sense should be expressed.

There is no question that it does happen. But the issue comes down to whether two people are expressing their love for each other or seeking to prove it. When two people are struggling with the emotional conflicts about love and whether it is or isn't for them, then premarital sex can be a booby trap. Sex cannot be the final determinant of love; it cannot be used to prove anything other than the ability of each partner to function and assuage sexual drive. Love has to be determined on the totality of the worth each feels for the other — sex only becomes meaningful and "proves something" when these other values are declared and accepted by both.

In a world where love and sex are confused, Joan Beck put across some wise thoughts on the matter in an article printed in the *Chicago Tribune.*

> The erotic is not the equivalent of the romantic (emotionally), no matter how tantalizing, and sex is not love, no matter how fascinating.
>
> But today it just does seem chic — radical chic, apocalypse chic, academic chic, artsy chic — to talk about love, to fall in love, to be in love. The concept of love, even the word itself, seems inexplicably alien to most contemporary human behavior cults and philosophies where relationships between human beings are seen in terms of transactional analysis, games and encounter. What happened to love?
>
> Maybe too many of us are growing up scared of the caring and the commitment, the for better or for worse. Perhaps we've made it too easy, too popular, to settle for the sensations of sex, for the "meaningful relationship" that avoids commitment, and for the emphasis on self that becomes selfish and self-limited . . . certainly we need to celebrate love more, to sing about it, write about it, talk about its infinite varieties . . . love, that many-splendored thing, love that makes the world go around, love that bears all things, hopes all things, deserves no less.[1]

That is why Doug posed that big question to himself and Midge: "Can I walk away from her and be happy? Can I walk away from her and face the fact that I shall never see her again, not share with her my life, my ambitions for God, my dreams and not know hers as well?" The man wants that woman to face it with him. That does not mean he does not have sex on his mind. He is no different from his secular peer in this regard. If he had to, he could rationalize his premarital sex test as well as his secular counterpart. He struggles with his sexual need and seeks outlet for it; but at the same time he has a sense of spiritual character that forbids him from dallying in promiscuous experiences. On the one hand, he is a man — ready, willing, and capable, driven many times to sexual expression; but he is, at the same time, aware that it can be destructive.

Yet, some women will not face up to that question that a man poses as a test of love. Some feel that it will take both of them into an aside of "unnecessary doubts that maybe do not matter but only create in him a hesitancy and a second-thinking kind of attitude." But the woman who will realize that the man is making the question a proper test for their love and who faces it will save herself a lot of pain later on. By realizing that he does not wish to make sex in itself a platform for determining their future together, she will be less prone to give in to him as proof that she is truly a "compatible mate" for him in the future.

That does not mean it is any easier for the woman to deny that powerful sexual attraction, nor that she does not feel the same pull and temptation to imbibe in it. She too has her needs for fulfillment. She too finds it easier to yield to sexual exchange than to refuse, especially if she knows she has some deep feeling for him and he for her. In fact, the woman who is wrapped up in the mythical measure of a man feels strongly that whatever the question he poses about love, it can be settled once and for all in sexual fusion. She misunderstands, then, the conflict and contradiction man experiences in this area with her, at least a Christian man.

The woman who feels that giving him sex will, in fact, settle the issue of love needs to know the inner workings of a man on this point. True, once his conquest is made, he may feel assuaged and appreciate her for giving him that feeling. However, he then experiences a strange ambivalence in this premarital sex test: on the one hand, he has proven something about himself with her that seems to be very good; on the other hand, once it is finished, he has a sense of conflict in knowing that in winning over her he has taken something he knows was not truly his to take — at least not yet. Then he begins to wonder why this woman was not stronger to deny him, though he knows it is unfair to put that on her. He senses that though he has "penetrated" and she has yielded, she has allowed him entry to that hallowed place. With that realization, he does not feel the sense of conquest he thought he would feel. Man, for all his demands for sex, is at the same time peculiarly disappointed when he gets it from someone he particularly cares for, even as the woman may feel guilty in yielding it.

The case for premarital sex, based on the new era of "sexual freedom," does not come off that easily. The idea that because two people feel strongly for each other and have some kind of "commitment" to each other for the future then sexual intercourse is normal and healthy and a good test of compatibility is a dangerous assumption at best. It is not simply a case of spiritual hypersensitivity either; it occurs often in secular men and hits hard at the emotional balance of two people. A man senses he has "made it" with her outside the marriage bond. Something now has been completed between them, but perhaps too soon. She has revealed herself to him in that one area she has kept to herself up to now, guarded as her treasure for him when their union is properly consummated in God. In the complete knowing of each other sexually — before they have settled the other more important values that should qualify and define their love — they have both come to know too much of each other prematurely.

Some women feel it doesn't matter to a man spiritually or emotionally. (If it doesn't, she'd better take another look and reappraise him in terms of a life partner.) They feel that men are blasé about this, that they are quite content "just as long as they get it." This is not true and does man a gross injustice. The man may appear to accept the sexual fusion with perfect aplomb; and he may even go ahead and lead her to the altar. But later in the marriage tensions may creep in stemming from that first sexual experience.

Perhaps Andrew Greeley pinpoints some of this conflict and ambivalence when he states:

> Sexual hunger is not merely a hunger for the Absolute or the Real; it is also a hunger for union between male and female. Then it becomes possible to say that when two people (or husband and wife) who are deeply in love with each other reach the climax of their sexual orgasm, they have achieved something that is, in the strict sense, "godlike," because they have temporarily fused the Male and Female . . . similarly when two friends feel the brief but powerful sexual union between them, they are in fact experiencing a touch of the divine unity. It is not a trace of the divinity that should necessarily be pushed any further, but that they are capable of union with a member of the opposite sex reflects the unity of all things in God . . . it would seem to be that for the two people the proper reaction is neither to find a bedroom where they can have quick intercourse nor to be deeply chagrined at the power of their own passions; rather,

I think they should be grateful for the spark of the divine that is present in them and the revelation, however briefly, of the power of that spark.[2]

What bothers a man in engaging in sex with the woman he loves before marriage is that he knows that the "godlike" fusion he has experienced is something out of sequence. It belongs in the marriage union. It is a Christian consciousness that interferes with his sense of conquest and fulfillment. It is his sensitivity to the fact that he has in a sense transgressed what he had always believed he should have kept sacred. Further, he knows now that he has lost control of his manhood, not proven it; he has abused his own sense of character and violated the one he really wanted to protect from guilt. And in the end, unfair as it is, he resents her for allowing him that penetration.

The Christian woman needs to know that a man would rather be pushed off and denied than yielded to, even when love is strong and some commitment to marriage is there. It could affect his whole future relationship with her in that marriage, because he will never forget that she gave in to him when he knew she shouldn't. Years later, a man can nurse a private hell of his own when he begins to wonder if she would have yielded as easily to any man; or if she had yielded many times before him. Virginity is a lost word in the lexicon of modern sex; but a Christian man, once he has violated that woman's virginity, that woman who later becomes his wife, is never quite sure if someone else has been there before him.

The best way to prevent this is to come to an understanding of the ground rules at the outset. If a man and a woman covenant to protect each other from the experience, if their prayers are a plea to God to help them, they will have recourse to that inner strength beyond themselves when that point of no return grips both of them.

In the case history of the wife who complained that her husband was sexually inadequate, that he was becoming neurotic over it, and that from the very beginning of their marriage he did not have sexual power, the roots of that were traced to the fact that he did have sex with his wife while they were still single. Other men may have no such problem later; but for this man, it played on him to the point where he lost his power under the tremendous pressure of his guilt. It took years of counsel before the man felt release from that nightmare and the healing of God restored him. But these were matters he could discuss with no one, not with his wife nor his male friends. No man discusses his sex life with anyone; it is something he alone must live with, protect. He might have tried to express it to his wife, but he sensed it would only complicate her life, give her guilt like his own, and that would have been far worse, as he saw it.

Greeley says,

> Guilt is an easy substitute for a much more difficult and complicated response — the recognition that our sexuality represents undifferentiated power, the goodness or badness of which depends to a considerable extent on our capacity to both acknowledge its importance and to humbly accept our inadequacies to do anything but partially contain it.[3]

But in dedicating themselves to attempting even to "partially contain" it, Midge and Doug kept themselves from the ruin that hung over them. It takes strength, more often divine rather than human; but those who draw on that strength have the reward of knowing the true ecstasy of a wedding night that is complete.

Because what Shakespeare wrote in *Hamlet* is true:

> This is the very ecstasy of love;
> Whose violent property fordoes itself,
> And leads the will to desperate undertakings,
> As oft as any passion under heaven
>   That does afflict our natures.

Love does allow for sexual intimacy even in the courtship. This is always the tension factor for closed Christian minds, especially leadership who spend a great deal of time in preachments and codes that warn against it. If there is no sexual intimacy in courtship, there is something incomplete about both parties, something never known, something, which if not experienced, may prove to be the undoing of both in the sensitive opening hours in the marriage bed. The touch, the caress, the kiss, the long embrace, the explorations that go with a communication of love are not in themselves transgressions.

The young man who said he looked at the back of a girl's head in his classroom one day and "knew immediately that this girl was God's will for my life" is taking a rather impossible view of both a woman and of God's way of revealing His choice. A man who has that immature approach to sexual mating and who practices a courtship with a woman from a distance, "so as to avoid interfering with the course of God for our lives and to be certain there is no contamination of our spiritual characters," will get a profound shock at first encounter in the marriage bed. He and his wife enter as strangers into the union, at best, and without the preparation of the "intimacy" of courtship, they may find the "getting acquainted" a long and uncertain journey of fitful starts and stops.

Even petting is not a sick manifestation of incomplete sexuality; it does help both parties to come to an understanding of their own powers, of their love, of their emotional capacities. It builds confidence that what they have is right. But all of this must be within the framework of love, not in the context of pure experimentation by two people in early adolescence who hardly know each other. A Christian man and woman who know their love is deep and true and moving toward union have, and must have, the understanding that this expression is as important as their conversations together. They alone know the bounds of that exchange. They alone know the point of no return. But at the same time, in knowing that, they can touch in the full assurance that this is preparation for the "divine fusion" that is to be theirs someday.

Allowing for this sexual intimacy — and it will happen anyway regardless of all the preachments, warnings, and chaperonage — which does not conclude with intercourse, is allowing two people to communicate and to know each other. They come to a greater understanding of the wonder of themselves which brings anticipation of what the beauty of marriage is to be. And even in that intimacy they come to know each other's weaknesses, the sensitive places in their emotions, the secret fears that emerge only as touch reveals them.

A man is capable of such intimacy without demanding that the woman "go all the way." Women who think they cannot allow a man to touch because he won't be able to contain his sexual drive do not understand that he is governed by the desire to protect her just as she desires to protect herself. A man, if he is any kind of man, and certainly as a Christian man, does not want to jar her emotions or fracture her spirituality, even as he seeks to protect himself from a violation that will bruise his own character. If a woman will not trust him for that in courtship, she may then put him on a wrong defensive when he goes into marriage with her. A man wants to know that the girl of his life is fully confident that he has the strength and the will to prevent any violation of that territory she calls sacred, which is her sex. In like manner, of course, a man must learn not to push the barriers too far, trusting she will in the end be the safety valve for both of them.

Thayer Greene in his book *Modern Man in Search of Manhood* commented on this need for intimacy:

> . . . one does not become a secure, adult male lover by a correspondence course. One needs to touch and be touched, caress and be caressed, so that the language of touch and the body, our first and most elemental language, can be a source of healing and renewal. It is totally naive and empirically misguided to believe that someone who has been separated from his or her body and instinctual earthiness for twenty years will quickly be reconnected by the magic of a marriage service or a wedding night. Of course persons with such wisdom do not expect any such miracle and are prepared for a process of slow discovery. One can't help but wonder, however, what frustration and disappointment might have been avoided with a free and positive experience of the body in the early years.[4]

Sixteen out of twenty-five couples interviewed in this connection stated that their intimacy in courtship definitely helped them to understand their own sexual capacities. It did not lessen their respect for each other. There was no guilt in the intimacy, but rather a growth in the new knowledge of what God had given to them for a lifetime. Those who denied any intimacy, any touch in courtship, though they consider themselves happily married, also stated that they would not necessarily play it so "antiseptically" again. "We were afraid of it," one man said honestly. "And we never got over our fear of it for months after our wedding, having been brought up to view sex as something that is destructive rather than constructive. We needed to grow up more before our marriage; if we had faced our sexual needs and had come to know each other sexually more — not in intercourse, but in an intimate sense of touch — we might have saved ourselves the awkwardness we felt in our first months of sexual union."

Thus a man's love in courtship is characterized by conflict and contradiction. A woman needs to know that he is not a one-dimensional sexual being. She needs to know that he has strong sex drives and at times will be pushed to assuage them. At the same time, however, he has conflict over the use of this drive — when it is to be used; and when a woman yields to him, perhaps out of her own fear of losing him if she doesn't, he will sense more contradiction than affirmation in the act. Such is the state of a spiritual man, and perhaps it is the same for the spiritual woman. The premarital sex test, then, is really not his intent; but the larger question Doug posed to Midge is one that is.

Fortunately, Midge and Doug made their courtship one that kept all things in balance. "Sometimes the balance tipped," Midge confesses. "We both knew when it happened. But knowing the Lord as we both did, we knew that our human frailties were taken into account by Him. That confidence in His understanding of the humanity we both had kept us from getting neurotic about it and preserved us from any sense of misgivings in each other over it."

In any case, they both faced the big question: "Can I walk away from you and be happy?" Neither could. And they knew something of that *fusion* necessary for the marriage union. Now they are ready for that moment of completion in the final union, which is to be all the sweeter for their loyalty to each other and to God.

What then of the journey that is before them? For this is not the end, but the beginning . . . the beginning of what? There is a lot of fine tuning to be done, new secrets to be exposed about each other, new lessons to be learned. Now begins the measure of each in courage, patience, and forbearance. The test of knowing what love is has passed; the test of preserving love now begins.

6.
THE UNCERTAIN
CERTAINTIES
OF MAN

But man, proud man,
Drest in a little brief authority,
Most ignorant of what he's most assured,
His glassy essence, like an angry ape,
Plays such fantastic tricks before high heaven
As make the angels weep.

— Shakespeare

As Doug faces her now, as he puts the ring on her finger, looks into her eyes, and speaks his vows, Midge knows only one predominant feeling: happiness. Happiness in the sense that at last she is secure. All the elements of perfection are in him. She has won.

Along with those thoughts are, of course, the feelings of inner excitement about their complete union in a few hours which makes her heart gallop a bit. The flowers shake in her hands.

Beyond the sexual union there is the happy vision of children and a life of companionship with a man who fits snugly into the role of her long-dreamed-of husband. He is her strong protector, provider, one who will command the bastions as it were, man his castle, control his children, and captain his vessel.

But while "O Promise Me" is being sung in the quiet August

evening, with the smell of rosebuds and orchids lending an aura of great expectation over these two, Doug is not thinking about their future life together. Right now his thoughts are centered on how well he will perform sexually for his wife. As strong as love is, as assured as he ought to be and maybe is, at this point he becomes most vulnerable because of his great desire to bring his wife to experience the highest satisfaction a wife could hope for. He is now going through an ego mastery crisis. His voice shakes a bit as he says, "in sickness and in health," not because he is uncertain of that commitment, but because his mind is on the other thing.

Midge knows inwardly that Doug probably has their sexual union foremost in mind now, too. More than she perhaps. But she doesn't understand that he is really tense over it.

For a man, there is a strange psychological quirk that comes when he knows he must perform sexually in a way he thinks his wife expects. The sexual revolution has changed the woman's expectations, Doug knows, and rightly so. No longer does a woman have to face sex with a sense of not having to enjoy it. She knows now that she is supposed to enjoy it. If she doesn't, Doug feels, she will be frustrated — worse yet, it will put him down as a disappointing lover if she doesn't.

That same sexual revolution has now made Doug feel a bit apprehensive, because if he should fail, his own confidence will be shaken. Then the marriage might become what Masters and Johnson described as a "kind of duel being fought in the midst of a battle."

Their intimacy in courtship has assured them they are healthy enough and are mentally, emotionally, and spiritually prepared enough to get full satisfaction together. But only to a point. They have not proved it yet. It may seem an undue concern on Doug's part. But as a man, right now this is how he must demonstrate that he is truly a man. All the traditional definitions of man which he has learned and sensed tell him so. Women who say it is silly for a man to worry about how good he is as a man in sex do not understand how much that is linked to his own sense of self-image as a man.

This tension Doug feels is tied to the world of sex that has swirled around him in all of its popular usage. What this worldly view has done is make human sexuality all-important. Mary Perkins Ryan and John Julian Ryan, in their book *Love and Sexuality: a*

Christian Approach, state, "In this then sex has become something impersonal. It is sex in this impersonal sense which our culture insists is necessary to earthly salvation while our early conditioning and religious education have told us that it is a threat to eternal salvation. No wonder we have problems."[1]

Joseph Epstein clarified the problem further by stating:

> Perhaps nowhere is more asked of sex than in marriage, yet perhaps no other institution is less set up to deal with the modern sexual imagination. The ideal of the modern sexual experience is variety and multiplicity. But in marriage — theoretically at least — one person must serve where multitudes are forbidden. One's wife must not only be a good mother, cook, and housekeeper, but a terrific sex partner. One's husband must not only be a good father, provider and companion, but give full satisfaction at night . . . sexual satisfaction is looked upon as a right. . . .
>
> Once people suffered sexual shortcomings in their partners and, while these shortcomings might be difficult to live with, they were nonetheless generally deemed endurable . . . sex itself had not yet become a highly compartmentalized activity, like high jumping; medals were not yet handed out for performance; people did not as yet feel so clearly deprived, as they would later if their lives fell somewhat short of *The Arabian Nights.*[2]

Doug feels that pressure now, that in this new day of sexual enlightenment his manhood is on the line. He, like Midge, has become victim of the fallout of the modern sexologists' stress on "techniques" in order to bring full satisfaction in sex. What they have produced is the "tyranny of performance" as Epstein calls it. Doug does not know all the "techniques," but he does sense that he must *perform* up to expectation. In this, he may misunderstand what his wife expects, but it does not change the pressure he feels to fulfill his manly role properly.

It explains, perhaps, why a young man, caught up in the same pressure, gorged himself on Snicker bars on his way to his honeymoon bed in hopes of building up the necessary energy to carry out that performance. The fact that he grew violently ill before he made it to bed is understandable, though the bride was put considerably off-balance. Carbohydrates are great for the long-distance runner, but they have no effect on a man's sexual capacity.

Doug, even as a Christian, is like any other man caught between the anticipated pleasure of the sexual union with the God-given woman of his life and the nagging subsurface uncertainty about himself. Doug, who has kept himself from sexual encounters up to now, is apt to feel this pressure more than a non-Christian who experiments freely to prove himself. It must be emphasized then that Christian men have this time of pressure, sometimes even more than non-Christians. Man is a composite of emotional and physical chemistry subject to the same stresses and strains, and though a Christian man does have the advantage of a faith that can keep him from panic and even in the end restore him, he can still experience this moment of uncertainty.

Midge needs to know that while she looks forward to him being her protector, he now is looking to her for protection. Protection from the possibility of an emotional blow he does not want at the outset of their marriage. He does not want to fail her in any sense now. That is the man in him. It is a good man who is that sensitive. It is not a weakness in him, though he thinks it is. What this demands of Midge is that she must be prepared to give him the confidence he needs in himself and not lie there as the obedient, surrendered wife waiting for him to *give her* the delights he is supposed to. After all, she is not simply a sandbag to balance the bed.

In Christian culture, here is where there is often a misunderstanding of the verse in Ephesians 5: "Wives obey your husband." Too many women who do not understand the secret fears of their husbands on that first night — which actually can set the rhythm of the marriage for months or even years — are convinced that they are solely the *recipients* of what the husband must give, whatever it is. "Obedience" may be necessary in other areas of their marriage, but this is not the place. The woman, by her passive state in bed, patiently waiting for the "big moment" to occur, is not helping him accomplish what he desperately wants to accomplish. The more she waits for him to "perform," the tighter he gets, and every tick of the clock is a clanging epitaph to his failure.

Where a man should have complete mastery of himself with regard to a woman, he is, as Shakespeare put it, "most ignorant of what he is most assured." Right now Midge must recognize that, as Greeley put it,

However good they may be at manipulating a man's fears and insecurities, most women do not even begin to comprehend how fragile their husband's sexual egos are and how deeply they need the most obvious kind of affection and reassurance. It is a rare woman who can say to herself, "Culture and upbringing have made him more afraid of me and of lovemaking than I am of him. Every sexual encounter between us is more of a risk for him than it is for me."[3]

For Midge to say that as an "obedient wife I must accept his failure or success with me sexually as that which goes with the biblical demand and the for-better-or-for-worse resignation" does not help him if he fails in his sexual performance. The Christian woman, who is a *receiver* all the time in marriage and never a *giver*, because obedience means accepting, has a rocky road ahead in those areas where a man feels uncertain about his own sense of command.

In a *Reader's Digest* article, Masters and Johnson commented on this by saying,

How such conflicts are handled is crucial. Fear, for instance, impels some couples to minimize their dissatisfactions and to tell themselves that the problem will go away. A young wife whose husband rarely makes love to her may console herself with the belief that "nature" will soon assert itself . . . or other couples will become defensive about it . . . still others pull sex out of context; that is, they consider the physical act as something in and of itself, a skill to be practiced and improved, like dancing or tennis . . . to reduce sex to a physical exchange is to strip it of richness and subtlety and rob it, ultimately, of all emotional value.[4]

Fortunately, Doug and Midge developed a year of intimacy before their marriage where communication was present — honest communication. Because they did, they are in a position now to make that communication work. Midge will recognize that whatever his sexual performance, there is understanding and the ground upon which to discuss it and give him the assurance he needs.

Masters and Johnson suggest strongly that in these sexual conflicts "the conflict should not be one *demanding* versus the other *submitting* — it would and should be that of finding the best way to meet the needs of whichever partner was under the greatest emotional strain." In this case, it is Doug. Most wives are not prepared for the possible sexual failure of their man on the first night. They are not prepared either for the emotional shock he feels about himself that may put him off-balance for months and leave the woman wondering if it is her fault.

The two things a man wants more than anything from his wife in that first sexual encounter of their marriage are affection and assurance. In some sense he still wants to be mothered or, as Greeley says, "He wants to be mothered and seduced by the same woman." The rule of tradition is that a man must arouse the woman, if he is a man. But, at the same time, a man often is aroused to sexual performance as his wife *gives to him* assurance, confidence, and love which say that *no matter what, you're still my man.* There is no shame in a woman taking the initiative to arouse him sexually. In fact, her own anticipation of pleasure can be manifested toward him in tenderness and love-making. This is the combination that can and does effectively communicate to the man that his fears need not remain, that he is not under pressure. The Christian wife finds this strange perhaps if she is locked into the role of "total submission" to the man. If she says, "Love (sex) is his department and obedience is mine," and makes that the rule in the most vulnerable area of a man's ego or sense of manliness, which is sex, there can be a long period of painful adjustment, which sometimes is never fully attained.

Epstein says,

> Where marriage should put an end to men's and women's sexual strivings, where ideally marriage ought to be a relationship in which tenderness and sensuality find a confluence, each flowing into and strengthening the other, in practice it seems less and less frequently to work out in anything even approximating these ideals. How else explain all the adultery, all the sex manuals for married couples, all those dreary works such as the *Sensuous Woman*, etc. [5]

Midge and Doug now have come to an area that is a highly spiritual moment in their lives, not simply physical and emotional. Because the sexual fusion is something linked to the beauty of God in His creative purpose, it is that beauty each sees in the other that will enable them to find "confluence." It, therefore, must be handled as something given of God, the concern of God for their happiness. If God wills such experience, then both partners will see it as a value each wants the other to have. This, too, will allow them to discuss whatever nervousness each may have at this moment. And if the man can realize at the outset that he can share his uncertainties with his wife even as they lie together, and that *he is no less a man for it*, the sexual compatibility they both seek will emerge. But if the woman feels cheated, if she is embarrassed to discuss the problem, if she simply tells him to "forget it and get some sleep," she is throwing him back into a terrifying loneliness. She has then become a failure as a woman even as she may conclude he is a failure as a man.

That first sexual encounter may not ultimately be the gyro for the entire marriage, but it is critical to the man because of that old myth of manhood that says he must fire all the rockets the first night or find himself woefully "coming up short." A man who fails or suffers some inadequacies that first night and is not given assurance from his wife that love remains, that understanding is there, will fail repeatedly later because he is afraid of being ridiculed. Impotence often is caused by these sensitive psychological factors. And if there is no realistic, honest, loving communication between them at that point, he will never bring up the problem again, and their relationship slowly begins to fragment.

A man finds it difficult, if not impossible, to discuss his masculinity or lack of it. To whom shall he go? To admit sexual weakness to his own wife is to admit unmanliness, he thinks, which is to demean himself. His ego mastery is lost. He wants to run, to hide — and yet, contradictorily, he desperately wants to stay, to hang on to that person who has given his life so much meaning. The wife must be careful, then, not to push him off by saying, "Well, what's wrong? Tell me! Is it me?" These are sharp stabs at his already crushed image.

And here is where faith has its power. Here is where that spiritual sensitivity must come to the fore. Here is where spirituality cannot be divorced from sexuality. Here is where trust in God reveals itself in trust of each other. There is no way to bring spiritual ideas in as a solution to sexual function, of course; but they are all-important in unlocking the frozen emotional states which prevent that function. The couples who leave God outside the bedroom because "what we are about to do has nothing to do with Him" have not fully grasped what the Holy Spirit's role is in providing comfort, guidance, healing, and love (John 14). If love is to be adequate enough to overcome the conflicts of sexual experience, it must be nourished and fed by a divine presence of whom both parties are acutely conscious. This does not necessarily mean that couples pray before they unite in sex. It does not mean they sing psalms during their union. It does not mean that God's presence forbids various forms of sexual exchange that might be "out of line" with Him. It does not mean that nakedness must be covered, lest He see, as if He would be revolted at what He has created. It does not mean that all must be done in darkness as if this glorious union is not of light but of sin. (Though a man must recognize that when a woman feels she cannot perform in the light, he should honor her sensitivity as part of her own psychological make-up, not as a problem in spiritual enlightenment.)

The Spirit longs for that union to have the highest value, to give openness, honesty, love, assurance, and fulfillment. He can do that as the two people involved allow Him access to their lives in this area that seems to be "out of His province."

And all that is said here about a man's feelings of inadequacy can likewise be said for the woman. The case history cited earlier of the wife who was "exhausted emotionally" over the demands of her husband for sex needs to express that to her husband within the context that God wants honesty. A man who "commands" his wife in this way, even as Walter L. did with Gladys for years, may be doing it for a number of reasons he himself may not be conscious of: he may be doing it out of a subconscious need to dominate rather than as an act of completion in love; he may be doing it to show domination if the wife is better educated than he, or more talented, or has a career that brings in more money than he; he may, as Walter L. did, be doing it to punish his wife who has not come up to the wifely standard he has set, who is not, like himself, going all the time, rushing here and there, climbing with him to the heights of the popular social arenas; he may even be doing it because he senses the focus of the marriage is shifting from him to her, that the roles are reversing. All he has left then to declare his mastery, he feels, is his sexual power to get the obedience he is determined to have from her.

Now his "glassy essence, like an angry ape" has come to the fore, and it does, indeed, "make the angels weep." In some cases, the woman may not enjoy the sexual relationship at all when the demands are made with no thought of her needs for arousal. She may become frigid through this conquest syndrome and lose the ability to communicate this to him or be afraid to do so.

A man may not come to a realization of what he is doing unless there is a spiritual sensitivity toward his wife, even within himself. The value he senses he has in Christ is the reminder of the value he must place upon this woman who has yielded to him, who is being victimized now by his demand.

At the same time, the woman needs to realize that the sexual demands of a husband may not be rooted in any ulterior motive; he is just following his urges. This does not mean he is "oversexed." He may be striving for completion with her in the one supreme way he knows how. Sex may be his only way of truly communicating to her what he cannot communicate in any other way. If his sexual needs are characterized by tenderness, care, and protectiveness that come from spiritual values — and these he must uphold, they must both uphold — then there can be completion and fulfillment. But only the woman can know and sense that, because sometimes a man is too intent on his performance to think twice about whether he is doing it right and taking all of her feelings into consideration.

This form of sex, "this force and insatiability of our sexuality is not a sign of the disorder of human nature in the condition of 'flesh' in St. Paul's weakness, lack of integration, alienation," the Ryans state. If the man's sexual demands are a desire for completion with his wife, then "it is a manifestation of the positive dynamism of human nature, of the built-in energy of the human psyche seeking completion. . . .

> This view of sexuality is in accord with the consistent use throughout holy Scriptures of images of marital love and marital union to describe the relationship of God to his people, of Christ to his Church. The dynamic aspect to marriage — husband and wife helping each other toward fulfillment — illustrates, however imperfectly, God's bringing mankind to fulfillment through Christ. Marriage as mutual completion suggests, even imperfectly, the fulfillment of human persons, including their sexuality, beyond what the heart of man can conceive, which we hope for in the life of the resurrection, the perfect dynamic union in life and love with God and with one another. . . .
> Christians should realize . . . and hopefully that the

dynamism of human sexuality, as of the whole affective drive, reaches through and beyond human relationships, to God who "first loved us" and who enables us to love him and other people; He can hope for the complete fulfillment beyond "what the heart of man can conceive."[6]

The woman and the man come to a realization of these marvelous truths as they seek to complete their union sexually. The woman must not simply take a position of argumentation or deprivation. To fight him, question him, or repel him is but to complicate his abilities and his desire to be the man she wants.

If a man loses out in his attempt to fulfill his wife, to complete that union in ways he feels are necessary to complete his own image of himself as a man, his control of all other areas of the marriage will slide as well. A man who senses he has failed sexually is a man who is on the defensive, who feels he cannot control the course of the marriage at all. He will then feel inadequate in himself and become morbidly self-conscious of limited powers.

The man who was away from home all the time and whose wife felt she was running a boardinghouse for him, which was no more than "bed and bored," was suffering this kind of experience. Involving himself in business or social demands kept him from being exposed to the same limitations with his wife night after night. Wrong as he was to make the lack of sexual power the barometer for his total being in all areas of communication with his wife, he did so because he felt his manliness had sunk out of sight. The wise woman who can make this connection can begin perhaps to get to the solution. One wife in the same situation decided to be gone when he showed up at home. The shock treatment worked on him. Concerned that she might be "straying," he realized that the loss of her would be harder for him to take than his own limitations in communicating with her sexually. In her case, this method worked, but it may not in all instances. The wife may have to endure until she can get him alone long enough to carefully bring the subject out in the open.

Healing and restoration come to Christian couples because there is the confidence that healing and restoration are there, provided by a loving God. But first, one or the other in the tension situation must deliberately strike down the walls. Counseling and psychotherapy, if a man accepts them — and many won't — can go only so far. But when a man knows his wife is trying to help him arrive at that point of completion with her out of genuine love, that despite all of his unkindnesses in his fight to save his dwindling sense of manhood she remains concerned for him — not herself — that confidence can be restored.

For that woman fulfills those beautiful lines in *Othello:*

> Unkindness may do much:
> And his unkindness may defeat my life,
> But never taint my love.

There is a powerful amount of love involved when a woman responds like this, and a man longs for that kind of love and assurance. And he must exhibit the same sensitivity toward her. Sexual satisfaction is one part of this expression, but it is not everything. Many a woman is quite content with the touch, the caress, the embrace which accompany sexual union, even when the man does not complete the union to the extent *he thinks* she needs, and a man needs to know that.

"The real issue," as Masters and Johnson put it, "isn't making love; it's feeling loved." A man's sexual drive is in *making love* to the extent that the bells are ringing, the rockets exploding, and the wife is in sheer ecstasy. That is the myth he has nursed since he was conscious of his manhood; that is what he picked up in the locker rooms of his life. The woman, however, who may not have all that glorious eruption in the sexual act but who, nevertheless, feels she is loved by her husband, no matter how imperfect the completion of the *act*, knows her measure of content. If a man can get that truth driven home to him, and sometimes it's the wife who can give him that assurance, a lot of the tension and fears will be diminished.

Norman M. Lobsenz and Clark W. Blackburn offered this advice in their book *How to Stay Married:*

> Without communication the spouse may feel rejected. But if the situation is explained, understanding can help to overcome the problem of the moment and restore sexual life to its normal vigor more quickly. It requires forebearance and love to avoid using sex as a weapon. (Or for that matter as a final test of the compatability of two people.) It demands intelligence to realize that the sexual side of one's marriage — no matter how good it may be — is not going to resolve nonsexual problems in the marriage. It takes a strong sense of emotional security to avoid

the mistake of equating sexual activity with masculinity or femininity. It takes time, empathy, a willingness to experiment, and a relaxed atmosphere before a husband and wife achieve a fully satisfying sex life.[7]

The fact that Christian men and women grow up without greater exposure to sexual expectation or nonexpectation, either at home or in their Christian education, is all the more reason for this emphasis. It is also true that a Christian man or woman may have taken on any number of guilt feelings about their sexual lives, especially if their "education" has centered on the prohibitions concerning any part of it. Therefore, it may take more time to negotiate the first encounter, but during that time there must be a readiness to discuss it, share the fears, and provide assurance for each other.

It is for this reason that the spiritual value cannot be left outside the bedroom door. It is that value which places the highest good on the other from which true love and honesty emerge. Spiritual value says that failure in sex does not destroy the man nor the love that brought two people together.

To leave the sexual arena with only a brief touch on the minimal possibilities and complications may seem to oversimplify the importance of it. But sex, after all, does not play the total role in the mystery of man. There remain those other areas where ego mastery suffers in like manner and thrusts itself to the center of the stage.

7.

WINNING — MAN'S DESPERATE SEARCH FOR IDENTITY

A man without one scar to show on his skin,
that is smooth and sleek with ease and home-
keeping habits, will undertake to define the
office and duties of a general.

— Plutarch

"Look, it's only a game!"

"What do you mean, *only?*" he defended.

"So they blew the silly football game in the last three seconds by missing a field goal. So life goes on, right?"

"Those are the Chicago Bears, remember, a chance to be in first place — "

"So Chicago is still there, right? It hasn't fallen into Lake Michigan and disappeared. Anyway, I am sure the Bears will get over it."

"They didn't need to blow it like that," he muttered.

"Well, the way the furniture is thrown around in this room, it's hard to believe they could have blown it. How many blocks did you throw in trying to help them today?"

"I mean they didn't need to lose — "

"So I didn't need to break my leg last spring either, but I did.

Some things change even when they are not supposed to." She laughed, because to her it was funny and because he looked so much like a stray cat right then. "So how about changing clothes and getting ready for church?"

He is not ready for church. He is ready for a good night of depression. Some men are hard losers. Some men manage to accept it, depending on what's on the line for them. But no man, as General George Patton put it, "ever lost and laughed." So Doug will go to church, but he won't hear much of the sermon, because "Blessed are the poor in spirit," the sermon of the evening, though quite fitting in a way, does not ease that lingering sense of defeat.

Losing, whether it be his own loss or the loss of his favorite team, can be demolishing to a man, sometimes even affecting his attitude in all the other areas of his life.

Some men will sulk for days when their team loses.

Some will go into quiet rages, and the family knows enough to walk softly around the house and ask no unnecessary questions, if any at all.

Some men will gorge themselves on fancy foods to try to assuage their mortification.

Some men will take a "quick two-day vacation" at the cabin alone to lick their wounds.

Some men kick the dog, throw out the cat, and write a five-page letter to their congressman that is a panegyric on the curse of taxes.

There's a lot to be said for being a "good loser," of course, and most men eventually find themselves swallowing the bitter taste of it and pushing on to the next challenge. Those who take their losses hard, however, are not necessarily immature men. Mostly they are highly competitive, striving men who throw themselves into every challenge in life with all the gusto and muscle they have. Their competitiveness does not allow for losing, because for them it is the winning that counts.

Doug's sensitivity about losing does not make him less of a Christian either, and at times Midge can come too close to laying that on him falsely. Doug is no different from a non-Christian in wanting to win; he has the same drive to run for the wire, to excel, to claim the victory. He is no different from Paul who said, "I press on toward the goal to win the prize for which God has called me heavenward in Christ Jesus" (Philippians 3:14 NIV). Or again, as he said it, "Do you not know that in a race all the runners run, but only one gets the prize? Run in such a way as to get the prize" (1 Corinthians 9:24 NIV). The Christian man, who knows he is in a competitive contest with the devil for the souls of men, is not about to feel at ease when he loses. And to divorce that attitude from that same man's sense of winning, even in terms of his favorite football team, is to make a clumsy distinction.

If there is anything to be said in the comparison, it is that Doug will have to be mindful to compete for the glory of God as much as he does for the Chicago Bears. But he alone is the judge of his values in that regard.

Some wives, however, find it almost intolerable to live with a man who is forever going through these "winning-losing" crises. Some find it almost unbearable that he must watch every athletic contest on TV as if his entire manhood were on the line in the winning of the Super Bowl. Some wives do not understand why a man will cut important business meetings at times just to get in on a John Wayne movie, or why he goes "bananas" over "The Bionic Man." (He does not feel the same about "The Bionic Woman," however.) Old war movies that depict an era during which he may have had a part, as sordid as they are, are also on his viewing schedule, because for him it was a time of winning perhaps.

During "John Wayne Week" on a local station a wife complained, "I had to serve his dinner on a tray in his study to make sure he did not miss one scene of action."

Sometimes a wife mistakenly feels this is a "regression to childish fantasy" and ridicules him for it. She will nag him or scold him even more if he chooses the John Wayne movie over a committee meeting at church.

Men have gone through all types of experiences to attain their own sense of image as a man, and that is what much of this is all about. This is true because there are no areas in modern American society where a man can test himself and prove himself as masculine. He may have all the biological qualifications for manhood, but to reinforce his *masculinity* is something else. The woman, on the other hand, can find her identity much easier in what are women's activities, and she does not feel the same pressure to prove her femininity.

From the first urge as a boy in early adolescence, he looks for the challenges that will help him emerge into manhood. In more primitive societies in ages past or in those that practice such rites today, initiation for a boy coming into the tribe were strong affirming experiences of his manhood. These "rites of passage" led to his acceptance as a man and settled once and for all whether he had the sap flowing in him that made the distinction complete between himself and a woman.

For the adolescent trying to move to manhood in modern American society, only the athletic department of his school offers him any hope. If he has some gifts for athletics, he can come to some sense of validation. If he does not, he remains "outside" trying to find other areas where his need for manly emergence can be found. Athletics is a narrow and limited field for all the striving millions of adolescents in this country who yearn to show their stamina, to pass the test of their nerve, and to gain acceptance from their peers and their superiors. But whether a boy makes it in athletics or not, that is still the arena where the real heroes are made (or so he is taught to believe). All his life he will find in sports or in the Olympics — that tense competition, body versus body, brawn versus brawn — some kind of identification either with what he missed or what he once had.

Without these adolescence tests of manhood, there are not enough areas to build a transition from the mother influence, which is essential if he is to find his identity as *masculine*.

> Boyhood is a time when ties of dependent need upon the nurture and support of the mother are extremely powerful, more so than most males young or old wish to admit . . . the mother continues to have a 'special' place in the psychology of the son, hence the importance of some process that will effectively cut the psychic umbilical cord between mother and child, as the obstetrician years before cut the physical one.[1]

If the boy does not find those areas that free him from the mastery of the feminine (motherly) influences, he may become hostile later in life toward women in general.

Sometimes this gets even more complicated in the adolescent experience within church culture. Here the boy senses the dominance of female leadership — women are his Sunday school teachers, sometimes all the way from nursery to high school, and between them and his mother's training at home concerning Christian teaching, he comes to sense early in his life that he is not finding outlets for the urges he feels to be manly. If the images of Christ, as well, are continually reinforcing those feminine images, through preaching as well as teaching, the boy will either succumb to a world of feminine dominance as being synonymous with Christianity or he will become hostile to Christian things in order to be free of them.

"Those who are raised as 'Christian gentlemen' and taught not to fight can testify to the barriers that this precept imposes upon masculine development," Greene goes on, "barriers that must ultimately be broken if one is to realize one's true self."[2] To the extent that there are no frictions and conflicts in a boy's life, whether in his church life or in society as a whole, there emerges a situation which Arthur Schlesinger of Harvard describes as the "bland leading the bland." It is not surprising, then, that boys will gorge themselves on TV violence and hit the movie theaters to view gory films such as "Jaws," because in that violence are the very ingredients of manly conflict he is being denied.

Then as a boy grows to later adolescence, his uncertainty with the opposite sex, as illustrated earlier in Midge's experience, is tied to his self-image as a man. If he has been in a Christian atmosphere all his life, an atmosphere that provided no test of his strengths and no challenging conflicts, he may never find himself comfortable in his own sex role. Sometimes these men will constantly back-pedal from encounters with the opposite sex, fearing they will be found less than capable of coming up to the mark with them as being truly masculine.

And, of course, though most men don't know the first thing about it, there is that chromosome factor. According to science, each person has 23 pairs of chromosomes. There are two sex chromosomes. The woman has two x factors and the man has an x and a y, what he owns as masculine, the y, and also what he has as feminine. Though not scientifically stated as such in terms of the psychological influence of this theory, this indicates that man is actually androgynous — that is, he has some feminine mixed in with his masculine. God put that in for genetic selection on the one hand, but it also would appear that He made man to carry both masculine and the so-called "feminine" traits as well. Perhaps it would appear then that God never intended a man to be "totally masculine."

But such knowledge merely seems to threaten a man. He fears the feminine within himself and will take his cue from women as to what traits of personality are strictly theirs. Once knowing this, he will work, sometimes relentlessly, to repress any of these within himself. The fear of showing any femininity — as our culture labels that term — can drive him to extremes.

Greene points out,

> Anything that even hints at the presence of "feminine" qualities and characteristics in behavior, bodily movement, and reactions of a man is enough to set off a three-alarm bell of anxiety. Frequently a man who has such repressed fears about his male role and identity will be driven compulsively to build his muscles, collect guns, seduce women, drive fast cars, or whatever may provide clear external reassurance against the inner fear. None of these activities need be such a defense, but very often they are.[3]

Such traits as sensitivity to others, confession of human weakness, tears, tenderness — these can be learned, *if a man wants to.* But fearing that these dilute his masculinity, he will practice the "stiff upper lip" instead and hopefully demonstrate that there is "no woman" in him.

Such expressions among military men as "never apologize for anything, it's a sign of weakness" stems from this insistence of man to keep himself "purely masculine." In like manner, a man will hide tears; in fact, he will go to great length to do so. He may sit through a moving, tear-jerking TV play with his wife and family. While they hunt for the Kleenex to wipe their eyes, he will do everything to cover his own emotions. He will yawn (trying to show disinterest), he will cough and clear his throat, and if all else fails, he will go to the fridge and spend a lot of time trying to find a Coke. To him, the showing of tears is feminine and, therefore, a sign of weakness in himself.

Some men are actually afraid that if they don't suppress these reactions they may begin to exhibit homosexual tendencies or images. The fear is real. It may be unfounded, but it is there nevertheless. Their "ego mastery" must be demonstrated; they must prove their masculine powers. And so these powers can best be demonstrated by the purely physical.

Sometimes this can be directly traced to childhood upbringing.

When boys in early adolescence have a muddy father image, when the father abdicates his responsibility for providing tests for his son in *all the elements of true manliness,* the question of emerging identity is even more acute. This is too often the case in Christian homes. Many times as the boy grows older the question he will ask is, as Greene says, "Am I the man my father should have been or that my mother wants me to be?"

The tests a boy had in years gone by to arrive at manhood are not present in modern American society. Physical strength, as the key test, is no longer a man's greatest asset. And though the physical is not the true test of masculinity, it is still difficult to define manliness for a boy or a young man in terms of character or spirituality or even intellect alone. This is where the rub lies. Today, job and environment put more stress on brains than brawn, on technical expertise or the ability to form strategies or design elements in keeping with a highly sophisticated electronics age. There are few situations left that call for the exertion of the attributes that prove and test a man's mettle. In generations past, man stayed alive by his ability to plow the field, put in a crop, cut down forests, and battle all the elements of a harsh environment. Manhood was presumed in terms of the physical aspects of masculinity. If the "stuff was not there" — the ability to swing an ax, plow a field, build a house, etc. — survival was questionable.

The "sixties revolution," however, found the young moving in hostile retaliation against those who had a much more "glorious past." This generation could not find their identity in those purely physical tests of manhood. Their heroes were not readily discernible, because no one was really sure what was the final proof of a man in the new society. In their frustration, their only relief was to attack the "establishment" who represented something they could not find.

Knowing all this helps a wife understand why her husband is glued to Monday night football, as well as Saturday and Sunday, or to those John Wayne movies. Through television, a man can experience vicariously what he feels he has not attained for himself as a man or what other generations seemed to have attained. If he does not feel he is an authority figure, either at home or on the job, he will then rely more and more on those reflected images, which say to him, "There is what you could have been." Or if his delusion is allowed to possess him, those images will say, "This is what you are." Greene explains this "delusion" when he says,

> This drive toward meaning and self-realization that underlies the growth movement of normal human personality could be described in one way as the hunger to be a hero. At first glance one might reject the notion that modern man with a certain measure of sophistication had any longing or illusions about playing the hero . . . yet one is on dangerous ground indeed if he dismisses what may only be hidden in the inner world of fantasy or may be buried out of sight in the unconscious. . . . It is a good rule to remember that humans bear a certain resemblance to the make-up of a floating iceberg. Only one-eighth of the totality shows above the surface. . . . So it is with the inner longings and images that may have great influence upon our lives. [4]

It is this part that is not "on the surface" in a man that baffles the women. In light of this it is easier to understand the man in the case history referred to earlier in the book, who threw himself into every community activity, so much so that he neglected his wife and family. He eagerly seized every challenge as an opportunity to prove his own sense of masculinity. Building tot lots, driving a tank on the Fourth of July, becoming a volunteer fireman brought to him the "tests" that helped him to find his identity as a man. (At least in the terms he presumed defined manhood.) His wife could not know this, and he would never tell her — he probably would not know how. But if she had known what was driving him, perhaps she might have been able to make him understand that it wasn't necessary to prove his manliness in that way. He might listen to her; he might not. But until a man finds this out for himself, he will go on flinging himself at these challenges, because they do give him a sense of manhood that perhaps was denied him earlier in life.

This striving for masculinity also explains why a 142-pound man bought two 25-pound dumbbells to begin developing his biceps as promised in the Charles Atlas book "crash course." Despite the warnings of his wife that for a man "who had not done much more than lift one knee over the other in nine years, lifting 50 pounds could bring quite a crash at that," he pushed ahead. For he believed this would at least bring him the image he needed as a man. What he received was even more than his wife warned him about; for as he lifted those two dumbbells over his head, he came crashing to the floor with the sound of a sapling snapping in two. The two dumbbells flew through a window, and he wound up with a double hernia. "Did you really have to?" his wife moaned over him. And, despite the pain and the embarrassment, the answer was "yes." For what did he prove sitting behind an accountant's desk all week? While astronauts soared to the moon, Joe Namath ran another touchdown on painful knees, and Johnny Bench hit another homer to win the World Series, he had nothing but an accumulation of audited tax statements to testify to his manhood as evidenced by a genius with mathematics. A man conscious only of the physical dimensions that mark the measure of himself will go to desperate ends to "dare to do more" to reach it.

It explains, too, why a sedate, sophisticated, polite, gentlemanly, dedicated Christian businessman ordered a souped-up Honda motorcycle and had it delivered to his house on a bright Saturday morning. Along with it came all the "easy rider" regalia — leather jacket, helmet, goggles, and a pair of knee-high black boots. Fortunately nobody laughed when it arrived. There was a bit of confusion in the house, of course, as to why he felt he had to now make this grand plunge, but his wife was wise enough to "let him get it out of his system." It was not exactly becoming to a forty-nine-year-old bank president, but then he was right when he replied: "What is becoming?"

So the same afternoon, looking like a misfit traffic cop, he mounted his "masculine identification symbol" and proceeded with some ceremonial flourishes to try to kick the steed into life. For a full twenty minutes, sweating profusely, he tried to get that powerful machine to life. All attempts proved futile. Unfortunately, at this point, his wife committed her only real error of the day — she called a neighbor who was a mechanic. With another man in the picture sent to "bale him out," the banker's mood was not exactly sweetness and light. But even though feeling a bit exposed in his helmet, goggles, jacket, boots, and breeches, and suffering the bantering jabs from his neighbor who thought it was a "wild, simply wild" idea, he sweat it out until the machine was beating a comfortable, rumbling challenge. And so he mounted, squared his helmet, adjusted his goggles, stuck out his chin, leaned over the bars, and gave it the gas.

The fact that he never made it out of the driveway, but that he and the cycle parted half-way — he landing in the rose bushes with a torn knee and the cycle climbing the steps of a neighbor's porch across the street — did not convince him of his "folly of acting twenty years younger than your age," as his wife could not resist reminding him. As far as he was concerned, he really "did have his day," and for one glorious moment he was indeed a "man."

And it can be understood then why Charlie W. insisted on "doing everything around the house himself," causing the near breakdown of his wife, Mary. For Charlie, manhood was in "fixing it himself"; to hand it over to somebody else was to abandon what he felt was his sense of ego mastery. Never mind that the plumbing job he did ended in a flooded basement; never mind that the sixty-foot tree he decided to cut down himself wound up with a limb going through his garage roof; never mind that the raccoon escaped him; never mind all the hospital bills for all the effort. For Charlie W., to his dying day when that tractor turned over on him, this was his way of winning. And this, then, was his "rite of passage" to true manhood. The wife who missed these reasons for his actions, or who didn't bother to try to find out, only added unnecessary tension for herself and him. It is the wise woman who will learn to indulge these strivings for manliness and not simply view them as "ridiculous, stubborn childishness." If she does indulge and understand, she will find peace with her man. Sometimes, of course, it does get embarrassing; sometimes it does cost in terms of wasted temper and money; sometimes it becomes irritating. But the husband "must have his day," his opportunity to win at something or to share in the winning of something.

Wives, for the most part, want their husbands to win. Men know they must win because their own wives find in them a masculine authority figure in that winning. Judy Garland, whose life with a half-dozen husbands ended in tragedy, may not be the most credible source on this point, but she did make one appropriate statement in an article she wrote for *Coronet* magazine titled "How Not to Love a Woman":

> We women must know beyond doubt that we're safe with you men. That you can take it, that you care enough to win. We will seem to be fighting you to the last ditch for final authority. But

in the obscure recesses of our hearts, we want you to win. You have to win. For we really aren't made for leadership. It's a pose.

Now undoubtedly that does not hold true as much any more as a result of the modern feminist movement, but many men don't know it yet. And until they are convinced otherwise — and that may never come about — they will press on to win. It is not so much winning at someone else's expense, but winning at those things he considers necessary to accomplish to bring out his masculinity. If the wife will not fight him on that, but encourages him to face those challenges and even stand with him in some of the struggles that go with them, she can know something of a unity with her husband that can be found nowhere else in the marriage bond.

This issue is vital, not only because the man is fighting to find his identity in a world that won't allow him the tests to help him, but because if he doesn't he may slip into crippling boredom. Boredom is a kissing cousin of depression. The case history referred to earlier about the husband who came home dragging, ate his supper in silence, found his TV chair, watched through the ten o'clock news, and then went to bed without his wife is a study in boredom. Even his communication with his wife sexually no longer had interest for him, as she was careful to point out, though it was not boredom with his wife that was the primary cause.

Actually in this case it was an increasing sense of dullness with his job as a high school English teacher. In that area he ran out of challenges. There is no question at all that it takes manliness to make English come alive for high school kids. But this man had come to a routine cycle of lectures and exams. Though he made a living at it and never knocked his profession, deep within him there was a growing exhaustion with the humdrum familiarity of it.

Many men who go through this do not know how to express what they feel to their wives. They don't even want to talk about it. A man does not want to admit that he's whipped in his job, for that is a kind of admission of defeat. Even when he knows that his disenchantment with the job, his growing boredom, is detrimental to his family, he will remain silent — nursing it, afraid of it, trying to hide it and hide from it.

Karen Peterson, columnist for the *Chicago Tribune*, wrote on the subject (March 1975) and quoted Dr. George Coehlo, a research psychologist at the National Institute of Mental Health, who said, "Boredom can be a veil for depression. It can lead to low self-esteem, a lack of self-worth and even suicidal tendencies."

Peterson also quoted Dr. John B. Imboden, Director of Psychiatry at Sinai Hospital in Baltimore, who said, "When we are bored, we want some satisfying activity which is not available to us because of external situations or our own internal conflicts. We are in a state of tension. Situation boredom can occur when we are placed in unchallenging situations . . . or situations that are too challenging can bore us too, burning off our interests because we can't handle them."

The wife has to be careful with her husband if he goes through this kind of experience. To nag him about his problem makes him retreat into it even more. To suggest he see a counselor or a doctor is a threat in the same way. One remedy, which has worked in a number of cases, is for the wife to jar him out of his rut at home. By planning weekends away from the "familiar turf," camping, boating, even just a weekend alone away from the kids, can do wonders for a man. Why can't he plan that or see that for himself? Because he is drifting off into a routine of depression and finds it easier to yield than to think of something he could do that might relieve it. "Man in a rut is as immovable to alter his state of drift as a cow in a mudhole," George Maitland, a counselor, once said. But it is amazing what communicating can be sprung loose from a man when he is out of his environment, sitting by a lake with his wife, away from the pressures and the factors that have created his depression. At that point he is best open to discuss his dilemmas, fears, frustrations, and boredoms.

One man, after his wife forced him to go horseback riding every Saturday afternoon for two months — she sensed he had always wanted to be a horse rancher instead of a shoe store manager — came home after one such afternoon, sat down, and said, "Honey, I feel like a new man. Something about horses — "

"I know, they have a masculine image, right?"

He looked at her in some surprise. "Maybe that's it, I don't know. But one of these days I'm going into the horse business — "

"Well, start planning now," she said. A challenge emerging is a challenge to be grasped. "I can put some of my salary into saving every month. With our two salaries, we should be able to swing it in five years, maybe less."

Needless to say, it changed his attitude. He now had his challenge, the one that he sensed could fulfill his search for identity as a man. There is nothing unmanly about selling shoes, but for some men it won't work. In like manner, there is nothing wrong in being a missionary, minister, or Christian worker; but for some men it won't work, and when they become bored in it they must confront themselves with the possibility that they did "miss their calling." A wife who senses this can be the key to her husband's salvation in a real sense.

The answer for him is not in asking God to change a man from trying to be a winner to being indifferent to the game. Nor is it to nag him about "being a poor loser" or "after all, it's only a game," thus depriving him of his need to be competitive. Some attributes belong to a man — winning is certainly one of them.

However, a man cannot remain forever caught up in the tension of winning. A man who simply cannot lose in anything or who will not accept a loss is a man approaching addiction that can be damaging. A man driven to win *all* the time can inflict harm on children who are driven by him to do the same. In the end, if it becomes too big an issue, any loss — no matter how small — will become personal. At that point, he is unable to function normally, because his world has become a huge arena in which he feels he must take on every challenge himself and win. Living with a man obsessed in this way can be painful, to say the least.

The answer lies in helping him to see the "other side" of himself, the side he refuses to acknowledge, the side he represses. He knows there is another side to himself but it remains his "blind side," because he wants that part of him blotted out. He is afraid of it. Call it chromosomes, the "x" factor, or the constant urge to exhibit his manhood or masculinity, but regardless, he will go to great lengths to suppress it.

His wife could help and should, but she must search herself first to see if she, too, is responsible for shaping him into a "male machine." Many women do not want their husbands to be anything else. There are spiritual principles for a man to follow, and certainly they were exhibited in Jesus, the perfect model of a man who had balance. Getting this across to a husband takes care, patience, and a certain diplomacy. Who else has all of these but his wife? Who else does a man trust more? The woman will have to ask herself if it's worth it, of course. But if she recognizes that her man can be more than he is in his extreme determination to demonstrate his male ego, and that he can be a far better man for it, then she will know it is worth it.

Maybe, then, it takes a bit more probing and some pointed questions: What makes him tick? What makes him strive to win? What internal and external forces pressure him to maintain his total manhood?

8.

THE OTHER SIDE
OF HIM — THAT
WHICH HE WILL
NOT ADMIT

There are some things which men
  confess with ease, and others
  with difficulty.

— Epictetus

"Why don't you ever play volleyball?"

"It's a woman's game."

"Since when?"

"Since it was invented . . . like sixteen-inch softball."

"I see men playing it . . . all the time."

Hesitancy. "Well, maybe they are so inclined — "

"To be women, you mean?" Silence. "Well, what do you say about women jockeys, football players, and that gal driving in the Indianapolis Five Hundred? You going to put all those sports on your taboo list then?"

Pause. "They should be playing volleyball," he finally says.

"And frisbee, badminton, croquet? They all belong to the women? What about tennis? Billy Jean King, Chris Evert, Goo-leegong — "

"Goolagong!"

"So? I mean, all you've got left that is manly is lifting weights, and only because women don't want to develop their biceps, right?"

"Not yet anyway."

"And that punching bag you've got in the basement? You look like you lost the first round to it."

"You are trying to make a point?"

"All right, while we're at it, how come you turned down the role as the angel in the Christmas play? There's only eight lines to memorize."

He is now uncomfortable. "I can't see myself putting on a lot of lipstick, mascara, and a wig, and most of all wearing that sack of a dress with wings pinned on the back — "

"Angels are sexless — "

"Then why don't they find a sexless outfit?"

"Like what? Unisex dungarees?"

"Well, I asked to play the role of Herod anyway."

"Why that monster? You can identify with him?"

"They can find a woman to play the angel."

"And we'll find a woman to play Paul Bunyan next year in the ice carnival, how's that?"

"Fine . . . after all, this is the house of the Bionic Woman, right?"

Another pause. She turns out the light and slides under the covers. After a long minute of silence, she says, "You know, you better start learning to walk on your hands." He doesn't answer. "Because that's about all you've got left to preserve your manly distinctive. You and the gorilla. Good-night, King Kong."

"Good-night, Faye Ray."

Absurdities? Of course. A grain of identity conflict in the man coming through? Without question. But as amusingly absurd as the banter is, something akin to it goes on in every home at some time where the head of the house is struggling with his own sense of masculinity. Man too often is stereotyped, and he allows himself to be. Men who believe the myth that their own identity as men must be defined in terms of certain activities, certain sports (as distinct from what women engage in), bulging biceps, hair on the chest, and oozing virility; men who feel they must be the gigantic, 280-pound football tackle, the rough-tough John Wayne, the calm, cool, collected astronaut, or even the suave swashbucklers whose masculinity is defined in conquering women are serving a myth that comes from historical tradition. But as long as the myth remains, women will have to live with it and them.

And too often it's the women who sustain that image, which is supported by the electronic media advertising. Female fantasies often center on these dominant, commanding physical attributes, fantasies carried over from the romantic literature they consumed as adolescents. The Clark Gables, the John Waynes, the Cary Grants, and the Burt Reynolds, whose flashing teeth and heroic performances have filled millions of miles of celluloid, have left an indelible mark on the women of America.

In early adolescence, and sometimes before, thanks to television, boys learn that physical power and brawn play a big part in influencing the opposite sex. The scholar, bookworm, or scientist does not create quite the same "flutter" in her. The whole process of balancing to this one-dimensional view of man is a complicated one at best.

Sometimes women do not wish to have any other image of their men, though they chafe under it. Charlotte Holt Clinebell, in her book *Meet Me in the Middle*, said,

> Many women also are threatened by a feeling man. We want men to be gentle, but sometimes we are too afraid that means 'unmasculine' . . . often in counselling sessions I have seen a woman react with anxiety when her husband was finally able to admit fear and let the tears come. As one woman put it to her husband after such an encounter, 'I like you to have feelings but I don't want to be married to a weak man!' Some women fear a man is losing his virility if he begins to have feelings and concern for other people. Women accept the dominant values of the culture as do men.[1]

A man, then, may be boxed in tightly by the image he sees within and the image propagated without. Sometimes a man secretly fears a woman, his own wife, and this will push him to extreme muscular exhibitionism. "Some of the male fear of women," Counselor Clinebell states, "stems from their experience of the shrewish and manipulative side of woman. Women do try to control men when they feel they can't get what they need any other way. . . . And yet I can't dominate a man unless he lets me!"[2]

Perhaps. But deep within every man is the very sensitive place that is forever attuned to the loss of his own controls for mastery. He does not wish to "dominate" a woman as much as draw from her what he needs to negotiate the pressures he faces every day. But the woman who becomes the driving force to him and pushes it to the point of usurping his powers, though she be conscious of it or not, will find a man becoming testy. No man wants to appear "henpecked" to other men. Women will and do communicate that when they are the aggressors in the family, the talkers as it were, the decision makers. It doesn't take long for friends to conclude who "runs the house" just by the way a woman may push herself in conversation in social situations. Men, then, will sometimes go to extremes to get that leadership back, if for nothing else than to save face as a man.

But apart from this, even if a man can find his identity as a man in other areas such as intellectual or spiritual pursuits, or in job situations that don't require a great deal of muscle, he may still drive himself to win at something. Many a woman can reason with her man that it is not necessary to ride motorcycles, grow huge biceps, or "break your neck trying to play football at your age"; and though he may listen and agree, he will still go on to prove something about himself as a man. To him, manliness is still tested in facing challenges and winning something in meeting them.

Charles Ferguson, in his book *The Male Attitude,* says:

> A male must demonstrate his effect, and promptly, either through bodily contact or through visible influence. He wants to feel his effect upon women, forests, continents, the public, whatever may be in front of him. . . . The male almost invariably attaches inordinate importance to position, to his own if he enjoys a distinguished or superior one, and to the position of others if his is lowly. He wants to have it known where he stands in relation to other men, and his standing must be confirmed by means of titles, slots, washroom keys, parking space assignments, classifications and possessions.
>
> It is a natural part of male behavior to note at once any outward change in the status of those with whom he associates, and to regard as a threat to his peace and prerogative any obvious improvement in the position of those historically regarded as beneath him. He resents the rise on any significant scale of those not his ilk, stripe, kidney, class, nation or race.
>
> With men an assurance of status has been long essential; with women it is likely to be imitative and a pastime.[3]

Even for the Christian man this drive can be there in his subconscious — the need for status, recognition, etc. He seeks recognition by his peers for his accomplishments, and love and admiration from his wife. A clergyman may fight as hard for this as does a boxer. A manager of a Christian bookstore may sense this need as he strives for new sales records in the same way that a politician chases the country for votes. It is for this reason that a Christian man's working hours can be just as harried by countless moves of threat and counterthreat. He often is caught in the same jungle of competition where he must, then, struggle to hold position or to gain new position. Those challenges may be good for him or bad, depending on his ability to face them, his emotional strength to withstand their pressures.

Such a man who comes home and is pensive, moody, and preoccupied is not at all uninterested in the world that is his — his home. Or his wife. Or children. The secret fears of what he might have lost that day before his peers, before his superiors, before his community are powerful deterrents to conversation during supper.

A man who holds this position as "bread winner" in his family is subject to a hundred shock treatments a day that batter against his remaining a bread winner. To lose in any aspect of that position means he is losing out in terms of his manhood. That is part of his "childish fears" perhaps, but it is a powerful, moving current across his emotions.

But these daily struggles go beyond the threat to his leadership in the family as major provider; they also cut deep into his ego. If he has lost a round or two during the day to others on his level who are striving as he is, he feels threatened. And this plays on him long after he is out of that arena, making him rethink and reevaluate, and in that process making him feel fearful of what is happening to him. Men who lose their jobs, for instance, suffer the deepest crisis emotionally, because it becomes a personal thing; it is an attack on their capacity as men to win.

A man has one image he feels he must project every day — that is, his image as a person of complete confidence, aggressiveness, and control, because these all go with his self-image of masculinity. He exhibits another image at home when he senses fear, anxiety, loss of control, and the specter of failure hanging over him, especially if he realizes he is losing out in his job or in his desire for peer recognition. When he continually pushes to maintain the one with all its manliness and fights to keep the other down, thinking his human frailties too "feminine," he suffers immeasurable tension. Sometimes his very survival as a man is on the line — he thinks.

This internal pressure and conflict will often lead him to withdrawal. He appears distant to those he loves. He desperately wants to share his fears with his wife, but this is that "other side" of him that he feels he cannot afford to open up to anyone. He sees these fears as a weakness within him and, carried out to its conclusion, a flaw in his manhood. This part of him is linked to the "feminine" again, for all emotions that are not manly must be the opposite. So, then, these are areas which he cannot readily discuss with his wife, lest he be "found out."

His wife would do well to respect his silences at times and not charge him falsely with disinterest in her or the home. A man bruises easily in this area of his emotional life, the area he protects the most against the scrutiny of others. The best thing a woman can do for her man at this point of emotional crisis is protect him from any pressure to confess it. She must have faith to believe that, in time, he will come to see that what appears to be a masculine crisis is really a part of the "thousand shocks that man is heir to." And in seeing that, he will realize it has nothing to do with a flaw in his manhood or something that is purely "feminine."

For a man to be able to cope with this, he needs, as Greene says, to become a "whole man — rather than a pure male . . . a whole man emerges from the interplay and combination of thinking and feeling, the active and the passive, the aggressive and the receptive, the 'masculine' and the 'feminine' within him. It demands much maturity and reflection to be in touch with both sides of oneself."[4]

This is when Christianity can play its most significant part in giving balance to a man, easing him in his conflicts about himself.

Jesus had several facets to His personality, but He did not hide them from anyone.

He could chase the corrupters out of His temple in righteous anger, displaying His manhood in what might be called "masculine" and yet later He wept over Jerusalem, displaying what is considered "feminine."

He met the challenge of the enemy and faced them in open

debate; and yet He could sit with children on His knees and in a moment of tenderness express how precious they were to Him and to the kingdom of God.

He walked the miles of bloody highways of Palestine, littered with the flotsam of man's inhumanity to man, pursued, harassed, and carrying a price on His head; and yet He could sit and allow a woman to wash His feet and dry them with her hair and rebuke those who thought it unappropriate.

He lashed out with a sharp verbal lance on more than one occasion, even calling the religious leaders a bunch of "vipers," thus taking the wind right out of them and leaving them dumbfounded; and yet He dealt mercifully with a frantic father who honestly confessed his inability to believe that Jesus could heal his son, touching that boy in tenderness, compassion, and power and making him whole.

He had all the legions of heaven on His side and could have, in one master stroke of His manliness, wiped out His enemies; and yet He stood mute before the Roman court, refusing to give dignity to a mob.

Here is the Son of God, Jesus, the Man, who was not asexual, but who never used His sexuality to prove His manhood.

Here is the king of the universe, sweating blood during the deep revulsion He felt in Gethsemane concerning the death that faced Him and yet pressing on to take that death on the cross without wilting.

There is no greater picture of the "whole man" — a man who was "masculine" in terms of strength, muscle, sinew, and courage and yet was not ashamed to show His "feminine" side in terms of tears, compassion, gentleness, and peace. He said, "I must finish the task," which in essence means, "I must *win for humanity* the redemption God designed through me." He won that redemption in the end on the strength of His *total manhood*, which was a beautiful, dynamic, sensitive manhood.

Marc F. Fasteau in his book *The Male Machine* looked to the future when a man would become truly *androgynous*, the integration of "masculine" and "feminine." He said,

> One day our lives will be shaped by a view of personality which will not assign fixed ways of behaving to individuals on the basis of sex. Instead, it will acknowledge that each person

has the potential to be — depending on the circumstances — both assertive *and* yielding, independent *and* dependent, job *and* people-oriented, strong *and* gentle, in short both "masculine" and "feminine"; that the most effective and happy individuals are likely to be those who have accepted and developed both these "sides" to themselves; and that to deny either is to mutilate and deform; that human beings, in other words, are naturally androgynous. [5]

The model for that type of man is not future. Jesus displayed it in all His glory, and part of His redemption is to display it in man today, now. Then why hasn't the Christian fully entered into the "balance" of Jesus as a man when He came to give man exactly that? It may be because he does not see enough of that manly Jesus coming through. Perhaps there is not enough preaching on the subject "Behold the Man" and far too much on "Hear the words that He has said." The words are important, of course, but they must be a part of the human, manly dimensions of Jesus.

Christian man still flounders — perhaps because there are no real tests of his manhood within church culture. The Christians in Russia know what it means to stand up against the state, putting their lives on the line for their faith. They have come to know what the true mettle of manhood is. But there are no such pressures for Christian men in America, no such trials of commitment, unless he deliberately forces those tests on himself. And few men are willing or motivated to do that. It is all very well and good to be charged to "stand for the faith in your secular office," but the pressure to do that is never quite the same as someone else forcing you to that test.

Meanwhile, he has only one recourse, and that is to try to make teaching Sunday school, carrying out visitation, singing in the choir, or taking up the offering the "manly Christian" activity. Though these are worthy efforts, they fall considerably short in helping him to find identity as a Christian man. The church, of course, cannot create the milieu of a godless state such as Russia in order to provide a proving ground for men. But leadership can once again recognize that a Christian man will respond to what is "manly" in the biblical record, whether it be Jesus or the rugged missionary Paul. If rough, tough fishermen could see in Christ the kind of manhood they themselves recognized and respected, then it is not wrong to conclude that Christian men today would gladly "pick up and follow Him" if He was thus presented in the glory and perfection and balance of His manhood.

If Christian men tend to drift from the false images of Jesus that too often come through, it may also be because of what Bob Benson pointed out in his book *Come Share the Being:* "Too many church leaders put Christ in a jar and put the cover on tight and pound holes in it so He can get air. And then they say, 'Come now, here is Jesus, come and see Him, but don't touch the cover, because He might get out into His world!'" And men come Sunday after Sunday and look at that jar, that theological container in which Jesus is locked. It is no wonder Christian men experience boredom and spiritual depression.

Until that "total" *man* called Jesus is revealed again in the churches, theology probably won't be attractive to the average man. He will continue to wear his mask, to project the one image of manhood outwardly and hide the other that is within. However, an understanding wife can remind him of who Christ is and how spiritually and redemptively He has set him free from having to play that "double image" game. The strength she can be is in encouraging his striving to accomplish but never pressuring him to accomplish. Or, she can complicate it even further. The wife who is not satisfied with her own status, her house, her own possessions, and who lays that lack on her husband and his failure to be a "get up and go" type, is driving him to frantic extremism.

The Christian husband-wife union often has these conflicts in the subsurface. The man who may be working in a Christian organization, whose wages are only average and who cannot expect to rise very far, feels this acutely. The wife who nags him that he "is capable of more than that" or "you don't have to take that the rest of your life" and "it's about time you moved up to manager, isn't it?" is feeding unwanted fuel to a man who does not wish to get locked into that struggle. Yet he knows what she is saying — that if he is any kind of man, he will do just that.

True Christian work offers the least in terms of the badges of accomplishment which the world holds up as proof of success, and thus proof of a man's skill and prowess. Unless the wife can come to terms with what he is trying to do in that kind of work — that he is trying to "serve" and to make his life count for God — the conflicts he faces will become far too abrasive for him to handle.

So he will wear his mask to protect himself. "Masks are necessary," Greene says, "and helpful when we wear them lightly, when they serve as bridges to the outer world; but when we confuse our masks with our truest and deepest identity, they become prison houses of the soul."[6]

Maybe, then, the wife is in the best position to try to gently get that mask off her husband and relieve him of that tension. If in their own oversight or preoccupation with the great doctrines of the church, the preachers and teachers fail to communicate effectively that model of the perfect man Jesus, and if the man himself cannot grasp that truth in his private spiritual pursuit, then perhaps it comes back to the woman. Of course, pious platitudes won't do it — and many times reminders of his spiritual heritage from her come as preachments and no more. But to be successful, she may have to confess to the fact that she wears a mask herself, that a part of her is never revealed to him either. While a man senses that confessing his conflicts is too "feminine" — because he has not yet come to full spiritual maturity in his manhood — the woman can do so with much more assurance. She has far less to lose.

But meanwhile man wants to win, and that includes Christian man. He wants to win for God; he may at times want to win just for winning. God does not judge him for that, and wives shouldn't either. He wants to win at everything that challenges him, because that is his nature. He does not want to win at any price, however. That is what makes him distinct from his non-Christian peers. Christianity does not — and heaven forbid, it must not — demand the status seekers, the position holders, the strivers for mastery and control over others. It is true, sadly, that the Christian organization as such has fallen into that trap. Thus, manliness for the Christian man is often best demonstrated in his ability to resist that trap and preserve the true values of Christ, even as Jesus resisted the devil and kept the glory of God intact. Ask any man — that takes guts. And if the woman will encourage him to stand for that, to face that challenge and win, as a proof of his masculinity, she will have done something that could well spring him free to that new sense of identity he needs as a Christian man.

Status, power, money, position — these things which ratify manliness in the world are totally contradictory to the kingdom.

Jesus refused it, even fought it. But a man may not realize that until the one closest to him, the one he loves, the woman of his life, shares that with him and convinces him of it.

Meanwhile, a man goes on striving for masculinity in whatever dimension he can find. Maybe the Christian tries harder. And in that striving, he may continue to indulge his hero worship of manly figures now lost to his grasp and whom he can never match; if he does so, it could be he has lost touch with reality in some sense, spiritually or otherwise. But until he recognizes the unreality of his pursuit, he may have to be indulged; he may have to be allowed his moments of sheer audacity to prove himself in terms of those inner images he feels must emerge to ratify his own manliness. He may continue to be a source of bafflement to his wife by his moods. He may be at strange distances from her at times. He may cause the foundations to shake one hour and lay a new stone in it the next. He may never be able to express the totality of his feelings, to be seen crying, to confess openly his human weakness and inner fears, because he thinks that is not in keeping with his images of a man.

But one day he will find balance when the man Christ finally becomes the center of his life. Some of his conflict in his pursuit of manliness will cease, although even then he will not completely withdraw from those urges to win. Jesus wants a man to lean into the wind, not away from it. Christ does not demand a display of muscle, but He expects a man to maintain his masculinity, to show courage of conviction, to stand against the riptides of life that would seek to destroy him, his family, community, or nation. A man, in this sense, will always want to win — but now in Christ he is not so concerned about the necessity of having to prove himself as totally masculine.

In the meantime, behind all the bravado, the will to win, the projected forms of manliness, there is still a man who is tender, sometimes frightened, sometimes feeling his own weakness, sometimes tearful (in private), sometimes angry, sometimes jealous, sometimes subject to all the human frailties of the flesh. But he will hold it together. God gave him the tenacity of spirit to do that. And what he can't hold in place, his wife, if she senses at least some of his composition externally and internally, will have to. For if marriage is anything, it is the mutual covenant to do that for each other. A wife who will and can live with him for all of that has accomplished something stupendous in her own right. But she does, because this is "her man," God's gift to her. The assurance of that has kept many a man from being torn apart by the conflicts of his strivings to manliness.

It is one thing to adjust to his demand to win. It is quite another if he is to bring coherence to himself, his family, his church, and his community, to face the other hurdle that he must take. The ability or inability to do so with his wife might well change the course of man-woman relationships.

For though a man can stand the heat of competition on the job and in environment in which he must grapple every day, can he stand up to the competition of his wife who may now herself be emerging into a new dimension herself in "his" world?

9.

CONCERNING LEADERSHIP AND EQUALITY — OR WHOSE TURN TO MAKE THE BEDS?

Press not a falling man too far.

— Shakespeare

He is proud of her.

Standing at the back of the convention ballroom and seeing Midge up front delivering a rousing speech to 500 women on women's rights gives Doug a sense of completeness. But while he stands there, the only man who "sneaked in" just to get a look during his lunch break, he feels a bit lonely too. She seems so far from him now. Seven years is not a long time to be together after all, not in the love they have.

But never has she been so free of him, so independent. Never has she charted her own course before. Never has she moved out into the world on her own. Always in these seven years, up to now, she has been content to live his success, his victories, his joys while enjoying her own motherhood and home life. Up to now, they have shared their mutual concerns about life, God, the things that matter the most between them. And their two daughters.

But suddenly it changed. He did not know when really. And he didn't mind it at first. As a man, he always wanted the woman of his

111

life to have initiative, some spunk, intelligence, a willingness to find her place wherever she could find fulfillment, even outside the home if necessary. Women who feel that men do not want a wife who is anything but a "house cat" have erred in their assessment. Many men are drawn to women who have strengths of their own. A man is not looking simply for a sex partner, but for a companion who complements his own drives, one who has gifts of her own that make him a better man.

Of course, there are those men who, in their striving to remain dominant, refuse their wives the opportunity of expanding their worlds. A working wife then is a threat to the male ego. These men cannot stand any "competition" from their wives in wage earning; a working wife is an "independent wife" — even though most women do not do it for that — and a man who is still fearful of his manhood will not be able to cope with the thought of his wife "making it on her own." This man does not realize that, by his adamant position, he is forcing the "separate world" mentality in his marriage relationship. He has little interest in her world of household work, and after a time there is a waning in her interest in sharing his office work, because it seems irrelevant to her world. It becomes a vicious cycle. In time, this "separate world" aura develops serious communication problems that can and do spill over to corrode the relationship.

Are there men who are different? Of course. Doug, as a Christian, knows something of human value, the value God has placed on a man *and* a woman. Doug knows, in his sensitivity to that godly value, that there must be sharing. A Christian man who has arrived at the proper God-given perspective of his wife longs for this. He does not wish to remain in his private world of job or secret ambition; he does not wish to withold his feelings about life — his life, her life — or the state of the church, community, or family. He wants to share his dreams, even as he wants her to share hers. Doug does not see himself simply as a watchman on the wall of his castle as guard and protector, content to confine himself to the role of detached observer while fulfilling the necessities of provender, sex, and shelter. For Doug, marriage has been a "fusion," a welding of the two of them as one; "separate worlds" is a contradiction to that fusion. Whether she chooses to stay in the home or later on find her place in a job, the Spirit of God keeps both of them vitally interested in each other's welfare, interests, and fulfillment.

This is not to say that all Christian men score high in this area of value for the wife. This does not say either that all non-Christian men are guilty of confining their wives to "their world" of household routine as is "their destiny." But what this says is that a Christian man is more sensitive toward his wife's needs, because he is conscious of how sensitive God has been toward him in providing redemption in Christ. No man, once having experienced this redemption, can view anyone, certainly his wife, in any other way except as highest value. It is the value a man places on his wife that determines his attitude towards her in all aspects of the marriage, including her need to find outlets beyond the home.

One has to sympathize, then, with those women who have gone to great lengths in their crusade for the "new femininity" or the "liberation movement" in order to get redress for their grievances. There is no doubt that there are "unfeeling male chauvinists." But men are that way mostly because often they can't handle the inner fears about themselves, their own manhood and how to demonstrate it. Whether men will be changed by derogating them as "chauvinists" is dubious at best. A man needs to be changed from within in order to take on new values toward his wife. Pressuring a man to change from the outside can only bring deeper resistance. It is, in short, nonproductive. The inner change a man needs is still the sole province of God Himself. When the Bible states "if any man be in Christ, he is a new creature" (2 Corinthians 5:17), it means that a man goes through a reconstruction of his attitudes which, in turn, affect his values.

This is what Doug experienced in his life. And because he has had this "inner change," he is not really out to fight women's needs to "find themselves as intelligent, working, contributing people in the family and in the community." Such a woman, who does find herself in this way, is a strength to a man, a proper compliment to him. He will encourage this, even if he does not necessarily deliver a mandate on it every day. Doug knows that some day Midge will want to get out into public life, into teaching or into business where she would be a great asset to anyone with her gifts and her intelligence. And the woman who makes a great issue on the subject is often beating the wind, because her husband is not in opposition. Most Christian men know the keys to a good marriage, and if they don't know them all, they learn well enough if love is there. These

keys to successful marriage are listed by Lobsenz and Blackburn in
their book *How to Stay Married:*

    1. To communicate with each other — to hear and under-
stand each other as well as to be heard and understood.
    2. To meet each other's practical and emotional needs.
    3. To work and play together, and to plan, meet, and solve
their problems cooperatively.
    4. To be close and mutually interdependent.
    5. To share the duties and pleasures of parenthood.
    6. To take pride and pleasure in each other's accomplish-
ments and sense of self-esteem.
    7. To be productive members of their community as indi-
viduals and as a couple.
    8. To respect each other's views, not to look upon a differ-
ence of opinion as criticism or as a loss of love.
    9. To argue without hating, and to settle arguments with-
out prolonged periods of animosity and estrangement.[1]

There is not a man, if he is a man worthy of the term, who does
not recognize all of these principles to be his own. He may not put
music to the precepts or sing an aria on them every morning; he may
at times be preoccupied with the pressures of maintaining the
household so that he may not always hit every one to the exact
dimension a wife expects, but he will still endorse them and honestly try to make them work.

Doug and Midge reached accord on these. They have added
one other principle: "To continually maintain the spiritual as the
enduring sense of strength and understanding for both of them, not
simply by presumption, but by an active spiritual exchange designed to enrich each other continually in spiritual growth." Because of their honest communication developed in courtship, their
growth in marriage, and their willingness to make the adjustments
necessary to keep the relationship finely tuned, they have developed a balance that is rewarding and fruitful. Their common faith in
Christ and His values and the spiritual force within them, that is not
something kept in blocked-out periods of time in their lives but
something that pervades their entire relationship, have kept them
from any serious fracture. Any experiences of disagreement,
bruised egos, or unintended thoughtlessness for each other have
been defused in their yearning to keep their union growing and
enriching.

This is considered to be the rare kind of experience in marriage, but only because so much of the broken marriage is so broadly advertised. Such marriages that are finely tuned do not make the headlines; the broken ones do. In other words, more space is given to the "wife beaters" than to the "wife healers." More coverage is given to divorce statistics than to marriages that stick "come wind or weather." When Zsa Zsa Gabor filed for her seventh divorce recently, the news stated that she had not yet broken the record of the woman who had accomplished thirteen divorces in nineteen years. But the press failed to report that at the same time a couple was celebrating their eightieth wedding anniversary. Divorces make news; the long-lasting unions do not. And because this is the case, there is more space given to what divides husband and wife than to what binds them — thus, the feminine drive for "freedom" has been fed by this distorted view of the state of the American marriage and the family. Granted that one in every three marriages is going through divorce — what makes the two keep going? The analysis of broken marriages is extensive, and the "incompatibility" clause has been picked up by women who presume that the wife suffers imprisonment in her own household by a man who "ruthlessly commands obedience."

What needs to be emphasized is that the percentage of Christian marriages that fail is much lower than others. This is not a "holier than thou" statement, but a worthy and important comment on the fact that couples who have a spiritual commitment are less prone to make issues of the "small stuff" and more concerned to work to make their marriages succeed. Perhaps Christian couples feel they have more to lose in divorce; not only because it is a loss to themselves, but because it is a mark against their faith which they have come to believe is the answer to human relationships in a state of conflict. And it is not true that the Christian wife must stand alone in her attempts to hold off the decisive fracture; Christian men are just as sensitive and aware of the need to "make it work." As was said earlier, a man will fight to hold a world together where he finds continuity and coherence.

The Christian wife, then, who states that "I am not all I was meant to be" may have a point; but the Christian husband, at least those interviewed for this book, is not turning a deaf ear to her plea. A Christian man, if spirituality is a vital force in his life, is anxious to listen to the honest expression of the needs of his wife.

Now in Doug's case, he has even taken the lead to encourage Midge to join a Bible study group, get some time outside the home, get some relief from the monotony of the usual housewife duties. Most men are more than willing for this to happen.

But Doug was not fully prepared for her decision four months ago to "get involved more seriously in community affairs," followed by "I am going to take that job the Republican Women for ERA offered to me. I start Friday." That was on Tuesday. If Doug didn't jump up and down and yell "Eureka!" it may be because he had not been aware that Midge was thinking of the big leap out of the home into an employment situation. But like many men who do not wish to puncture the balloons of their wives in any form, he simply gulped and said, "Hey, that might be just great for you!"

"Not only that," she says almost gloatingly, "it even pays well."

But there were details to be worked out. And Doug simply sat and listened, dumbfounded, as she checked it off. For the two girls, Kathy, aged 5, and Cynthia, aged 3, there would be a "sitting mother," a Mrs. Milligan. She could stay with the kids until 3:30 when Midge would come home. "By getting home early in the day, they won't feel lost or under new management or something," Midge says confidently.

Doug doesn't exactly know how to handle this one. He has some doubts, not about her desire to move out into a new level of life for herself, but whether it is the right time. Two preschool children need a mother for more hours then those allotted in Midge's schedule. Yet Doug felt no specific threat in what she wanted to do. He welcomed her desire for "equality." After all, they exercised it in their sexual relationship where Midge gave and was as much the aggressor toward him as he was to her. It made for a richer union without question. He welcomed her equality in the decision-making areas with regard to the home, the children, and finances.

Well, then, why three months later did he suddenly feel this strange "sense of loneliness" as he watched her holding forth in that ERA convention?

Maybe it went back to that morning a month or so ago, just after breakfast, when Midge said, "Doug, I've got to run . . . how about making the beds?"

"Me?" and Doug almost choked on his coffee.

"Sure," she said lightly. "You don't have to get to your office until nine. I have to be downtown by eight. Now don't forget Kathy needs her special kind of cereal so she won't break out . . . Mrs. Milligan gets a bit nervous when that happens. And don't forget to change Cynthia before you go . . . you know how Mrs. Milligan hates to start the day that way. So I'll run. See you later today, dear!"

So for Doug there has been a sudden, new turn in the marriage and family relationship. The lines between who plays the masculine-authority role and who plays the feminine are not going to be so cleanly defined any more. He's man enough to recognize that it need not be destructive. He knows that Midge is not the stereotyped "weaker" sex just because she is feminine. She is not boxed into that any more than he is in terms of his masculinity.

However, a wife moving out into the job market can leave some men totally disoriented. As Lobsenz and Blackburn put it,

> Some men are more disturbed by psychological discomforts. For a husband who identifies "having a job" and "earning money" with a strictly masculine prerogative, a working wife can be a threat to his ego. The same is true for the man who basically doubts his competence and inadequacy as a male. The situation is further complicated if his wife earns as much, or more, money than he does, or if her job has more status than her husband's.[2]

A woman needs to know beforehand just what her husband's feelings are on her moving out into the job market and taking on a kind of independent status. Midge may have failed in not preparing Doug for what her job would demand of him in terms of household duties. She had not shared enough of her desire to be out of the house, to be working, and the reasons for it, which in her case were simply a desire to be useful and find her identity beyond the routines of motherhood and housework. If Doug doesn't really know her reasons, he may begin to feel "put upon " and a bit threatened.

But Doug knows enough by his relationship with Midge that she needs more outlet. He wants her to exercise her keen intellectual powers, her gifts of leadership, her business sense. To deny her that, to protest, is to deny what their relationship has been all along — a willingness to share with each other, to allow each other to participate as they can together in life's challenges, or to do so separately. Doug knows that while he is out every day in the world, facing new challenges in his career as a chemist, meeting new people, gaining new insights into life and behavior, Midge is caught within the periphery of her role as a housewife and mother. Doug tries to share the important things of his life outside the home, but that is not the same thing as being out there.

So he knows that even as a Christian he cannot deny Midge her desire and demand that she "submit" to his own inner conviction that she not move out into a job yet. He knows that she must have her opportunity, and perhaps whatever adjustments are necessary won't be all that bad. But two preschool children at home make her decision a bit premature, and this is what bothers him the most.

So he makes the beds. It takes him a while, but he gets it done. He greets Mrs. Milligan and gives her the list of instructions from Midge. He kisses his two daughters good-bye and goes off to work. Fine. It all seems to be working. The first two months finds Midge in a whole new world of exciting happenings. Doug listens to her recount of her day and shares her enthusiasm and excitement. And he goes on making the beds. Then Mrs. Milligan begins calling him at the office at noon to ask him to come home and settle down the kids. Since his office is close by and Midge's is thirty miles away, he is the natural one to respond. So he goes home, plays with the two children, gets them calmed down, and goes back to work. How many times he will be able to do that without a lot of explaining to his superiors is a question.

But the day he comes home at five in the afternoon and finds Mrs. Milligan still there, looking grumpy but tolerant of the late hour, and no Midge, he feels that the controls are beginning to slip. By now the two children are crying, fighting over a toy. The place is in considerable disarray, toys everywhere, spare diapers scattered here and there.

Doug dismisses Mrs. Milligan with an apology, and she leaves in a kind of huff. He cleans up and waits. It is now seven o'clock. He has fed the children, changed them, and put in a pizza for himself; he can't cook anything else. He's not even sure of the pizza. He eats alone, watches the TV news alone. It is now 8:30. No Midge. He puts the children to bed. Then back to the TV where he watches a dull drama about a man wanting to have an operation for a sex change. He grunts. Then laughs. It seems to him now that a sex change can come much easier and less painfully. But he realizes that it is an unfair thought. Where is Midge? Has something gone wrong?

At 9:15 she arrives, glowing, bubbly, full of news. The ERA bill is going to the legislature. It looks as if it has a chance of winning. She may get to go to the capital as chairman of the lobby group. Ouch! Doug swallows but says, "Sounds great," and hopes it doesn't sound too flat.

Now perhaps he knows why the feeling of "loneliness." She is moving more and more away from him, from the home, from the central point where they have found their union to be so fulfilling and rich. Her work, of course, "is a tremendous opportunity for me to make an influence for women and certainly for Christ," she adds, just in case she needs a bit of support. How does he argue with that? Can he now say anything about "it's lonely when you are not here . . . it's chaotic in fact . . . there is something moving out of balance here, something going out of control"?

That would be kind of childish reaction to that sense of "needing a mother" again. He knows about husbands who need the mother touch. He doesn't think that's what he needs. But the pizza did taste grainy in his mouth, and the house feels as if it has been the abode of strangers. The warmth that it once had under Midge's control has about disappeared. A strange woman occupies it all day and leaves something of her character, personality, odors, and influence. The children are taking on her habits, her controls, her way of doing things, her commands for obedience. And they are somewhat confused too, not capable of making those adjustments.

Maybe now he can come to understand — though a bit abruptly — what Sidney Cornelia Callahan said in her article "A Christian Perspective of Feminism" in the book *Women's Liberation in the Church.*

> Women all too often are not encouraged to make life plans to consider the future. They are encouraged to live only in the present, to be concerned only with expression rather than action, and to be complementary to some man's life, rather than to live their own. Yet one's identity depends on carrying out purposes in time and being responsible for one's self. . . I believe Christianity encourages women to develop more initiative and responsibility. . . . After all God is not male or female,

but uniquely divine . . . in Catholicism Mary's importance can be seen as explicit revocation of the curses of Genesis. No more feminine subordination to husbands. No more pain in child-birth. No more nonsense about women being unclean and so unfit for the priesthood . . . the Magnificat is a proud soaring song, having nothing to do with passivity, sweetness, timidity or the feminine mystique.[3]

Well and good. But for Doug right now there are dishes stacked up in the sink, dirty diapers in the laundry tub. That is about the extent of his concept of the "Magnificat" right now. There is not much song in it. Rather, there is a discord here, almost as unpalatable as the pizza that still rumbles in his stomach. What Doug is feeling lonely about is not that Midge has found an exciting outlet for her life and less time for him. What he senses mostly now is that the one area where he can feel and sense continuity, order, security, and love is being threatened. He is concerned that a role reversal is forming. He is not particularly adverse to doing dishes — he's done them before for Midge. He doesn't mind changing diapers; he's done his share already. And making beds isn't all that much of a chore. But he fears that he is heading toward a demand to master both worlds — the challenges of his work in the office and the encroaching demands here at home. A tired man, a man carrying the weight of decisions not yet made at an office all day, pondering which way to make them, has no real "Magnificat" on his lips. What he has is confusion.

If there is a shift in role reversal, Midge moving farther and farther out into her world of involvement and Doug forced farther back into the role of housekeeper and child raiser, there is then a squeeze on his sense of leadership. If that role reversal occurs, he will have lost the focal point of the family, the marriage which has been his up to now. He has not demanded it, but Midge gave it to him when they married. He took the leadership, because it is his nature to take it, to accept the responsibility, to provide the necessary resources to keep them fed, sheltered, and secure. It may be that men are used to women being a certain way, knowing their place, putting the interest of their men and children ahead of their own, and allowing their husbands to maintain control or have their own way. For him to move over from that, to turn his back on years of tradition in one snap decision at ten o'clock one night, is presuming too much of him by any woman.

What starts out as a "part-time" job outside the home — and if kept that way can be done without shaking the foundations — in too many cases becomes an independent life style, a sudden plunge into a captivating world of excitement and involvement. When it becomes "full time," something has to give. Somewhere along the line of the marriage course, a fracture is about to appear. Midge may not be aware of what is happening. Maybe as long as Doug keeps silent, she won't. And he will remain silent until — and maybe that is too long — his sense of manhood is at stake or until his loneliness and loss of communication with her are too much to bear.

Doug wants to lead, because his leadership has given them a happy marriage up to now. Though it is not yet unhappy, he is not comfortable with the change of rhythm he feels in his own house. His leadership has held a sense of order for them both, and no man wants to see that order thrown into chaos. His leadership in his sexual relations was proven by his ability to satisfy Midge, and this leadership carried him into other areas where he could give her that continuing sense of completeness. Leadership does not mean commanding a wife; leadership means providing a channel whereby she can focus her desires, her ambitions, and derive strength to arrive at the realization of them.

In this regard then, perhaps the woman needs to know, because her case has been loudly and widely vocalized already, that a man is faced with dilemmas and anxieties over this shift of leadership. As Lobsenz and Blackburn put it:

> A man must be many things to many people: wage earner, lover, protecting husband, father, citizen of the community. He is expected to make a good living, give time to his children, take part in civic affairs, satisfy his wife sexually and help her with household tasks. Men in responsible positions are often under tremendous pressures. The competitive pace of business never slackens, and a man must continually produce results in order to advance. All these pressures put a conscientious husband under severe stress. It often seems to him there is no time for himself, that he is always at the beck and call of someone else.
>
> Yet there is one saving grace for a man. Our culture places one of his responsibilities above all the others: for the over-

whelming majority of men the primary function is to support family. Unless carried to neurotic extremes, the primacy of man's role as worker and provider virtually excuses him from blame for any failure to perform his other functions with equal emphasis or competence . . . this is his anchor.[4]

The wife has to make up her mind about what she is to be in relationship to her husband so he maintains some kind of leadership, if for nothing else than to preserve some order. Again Lobsenz and Blackburn sum up the dilemmas:

> For one thing, tradition urges a woman to be an old-fashioned wife; and it is glamorous and tempting to be a companion-wife; present educational standards urge her to be a partner-wife . . . yet [and here is the problem] many wives act as if they are entitled to the benefits of all the various roles — the security of the old-fashioned wife, the leisure of the companion, and the independence of the partner — but are willing to assume the obligations of only one. . . . And husbands often expect their wives to be all these women at once, submissive and aggressive, fun-loving and hard-working, glamorous and comforting.[5]

At any rate, the answer for Doug and Midge is that the extremism must be faced. Midge has opted for a careerist role over her other roles as mother, partner, and companion. The woman who does so, and who needs to perhaps at some point in her marriage, may find excitement in being so fully involved as a career wife, but she may never realize the erosion taking place in her marriage. The longer a wife persues the careerist role, the more enamored she becomes of it, and the less sensitive she can become to her husband's needs. A man's "loneliness" then is in the fact that he has lost out on his leadership and the attendant values that kept him fulfilled with his wife. In this he can only be pushed so far. With this, Doug fears *role reversal,* and no man is ever fully ready for that.

Role reversal trends are not rare or unusual. For instance, an article in the *Chicago Tribune* written by Ronald Kotulak (7 May 1976) indicated that a

> study of 140 college students, including an equal number of men and women, showed they prefer the nontraditional male over the stereotyped he-man (study conducted by Virginia E. O'Leary and James M. Donoghue, psychologists at Oakland University). The findings showed that the masculine stereotype

may be undergoing changes similar to those of the role of
women as evident in the feminist movement . . . the traditional
female role is changing so that college students now prefer
women who have so-called "masculine interests" and who are
more assertive, dominant, successful and competitive, they
said. The new study shows the ideal man is one who is developing more traditionally "feminine" interests, the researchers
said.

Perhaps college students, who look for ways to relieve their
frustration by seeing how many men they can stuff in a telephone
booth or how many raw eggs they can swallow in sixty seconds, have
not won the field yet for determining the style of sex roles they
would fashion. They have not experienced the marriage and family
relationship, nor do they understand the immense psychological
pressure of the traditional values of man-woman relationships. A
single man or woman can afford to play with these possibilities of role
reversal; a married man or woman with children has far more at
stake. This finely tuned marriage that has been arrived at through
years of give and take, sometimes marked by stormy nights and
turbulent days, cannot so easily be tampered with experimentally
without risking a domino effect that could abruptly rearrange the
relationship.

The case history referred to earlier in this book where the man
became totally dependent on his wife for all the decisions in the
family, needing reinforcement of his own self-image and his ability
to do his job, was in fact a victim of role reversal. His wife, who was a
much more dominant personality, took over the house from the first
day, eventually began working outside the home, and exerted a
command that was obvious to everyone except herself. The result
was that the man sensed a "put down," to say the least, of his own
manhood; he opted out of his leadership role — and who knows how
long he fought that — and finally took on the housework, finding in it
a defense for himself where nothing else would suffice. It was not
surprising then that the wife found herself with a man who had
become as much of a conundrum to her as to himself. To get that
marriage back on track and out of its lopsided tilt of role reversal took
three years of counseling, prayer, patience, and a lot of tears and
scarred emotions.

However, that study of college students indicated something

more than a mere campus egg-swallowing-marathon syndrome. It is interesting to note that with all of their disenchantment with traditional sex roles, the National Mental Health Study showed that 87 percent of college students polled list family life among their most important goals.

Charlotte Holt Clinebell says:

> Apparently it isn't marriage itself that is in question in many cases, as much as it is the limited models and cramping definitions of marriage that we still struggle under. People, especially women (but men too), are now looking for greater intimacy in marriage than formerly was the case; they are looking for more fulfilling life-styles, for richer relationships, for more human satisfactions. This puts a heavier burden on the marriage relationship, one that the traditional style of marriage often cannot bear.[6]

What the college students suggested in terms of reshaping fixed stereotyped roles of male and female may not be totally accepted yet, and they may be the ones to prove that it can be done. But what Doug and Midge need in this critical moment is to find their marriage moving more toward "middle ground" that will be satisfactory to both.

> As women and men we are in this thing of being alive together. Someone has said that blacks and whites are the same but equal while men and women are different but equal. As women and men we share intricately interwoven lives. We live in the same houses, raise the same children, work in the same offices and schools and industries. We must find ways of valuing and affirming each other and what goes on between us. . . . For centuries the "battle of the sexes" has revolved around the issue of dominance and submission, weakness and strength. What many women are now asking for is genuine *interdependence*, that is what I mean by the word "equality." . . . It is a sharing of the load, of the leadership, of the burdens and joys of being human. . . . The issue in equality of the sexes is not that women must become "like men" or that men must become "like women" . . . it does not mean we must give up whatever turns out to be our uniqueness as males and females.[7]

But where and when does the distinction fade and dissolve? It need never happen at all. There is here in Clinebell's suggestion of "interdependence" something worth pursuing in a rapidly changing

role system between man and wife. It is a means of avoiding a
head-on confrontation, splintered egos, unnecessary pain, and
perhaps, inevitable separation. "A sharing of the load, of the leadership, of the burdens and joys" is what Doug could easily and willingly accept. As events are now shaping in his life, he is staggering
under the load of role reversal, of trying to perform in duties at home
equally as well as he must in his own job. Though they are Christians, the nailing down of a proper Christian sharing of responsibility
is absent. Doug won't call Midge's attention to what is happening to
his own sense of self-image, while Midge, caught up in her own
euphoria, is blind to what has occurred in the relationship and is not
aware that the erosion of the union is already beginning.

What Clinebell is saying is that this "middle ground"

> means hanging loose about sex roles — what Maslow describes
> as "desexualizing of the statuses of strength and weakness and of
> leadership so that either man or woman can be, without anxiety
> and without degradation, either weak or strong, as the situation
> demands. Either must be capable of both leadership and sur-
> render." The different-but-equal philosophy simply says that
> where merit and opportunity are concerned a meeting in the
> middle is the only way we can be fully human together.[8]

Midge does not have to throw herself so completely into the
compulsion of a careerist wife at the expense of her husband's needs.
Doug need not be pushed into a sex reversal role either, and he need
not resort to a reassertion of his leadership and command and order
his wife to stay home "or else."

"Equal though different" allows each of them to find the outlets
that will complement their gifts and yet not disturb or destroy the
rhythm of the union already established. In this arrangement,
Midge could take a job that would allow her to be at home when
needed the most. For the children's sake, this ought to be the first
consideration. For the man, he counts on his wife's presence at two
critical times of his day — in the morning during breakfast when he
can share what he faces that day and can draw from his wife that extra
touch of love and encouragement, and when he arrives home at
night. A tired man, a harried man, who has been whipped by his job,
looks forward to that home when his wife has command of it, has it in
order, has permeated it with her love and structured it with his
needs in mind (as well as her own).

A man who can leave for the job in the morning knowing that the priorities are being met willingly by his wife, knowing she will control the household and be responsible for the children, is a man freed of a colossal weight. A woman, then, who can fulfill her *intuitive* role as a mother and wife and still find new involvement outside without threatening the balances between her and her husband is what "equal though different" is all about. Her role as wife and mother is still her focal point, while she fulfills her needs in other areas.

> Shared leadership (Clinebell says) is not necessarily 50-50 leadership — probably not even desirably so. Although the couple may choose to divide up specific tasks systematically, each is both free and responsible for pitching in when the other is under pressure; in a relationship where people are mature enough to focus on what's best for the relationship as well as for the individuals, the leadership is flexible . . . where there are areas of conflict and leadership does not flow easily, negotiation is possible while dealing with the conflict. Negotiation is only possible, however, when both are committed strongly to the relationship and its growth as well as to their own individual needs and personal growth. . . .
>
> Equalitarian marriage makes it possible for two people to be "forever friends" as well as lovers. But it requires a kind of openness and honesty and trust that are impossible in dominance-submission relationships . . . such openness means that we can give up many of the rituals that have defined us as female and male instead of as persons, and have therefore kept us apart.[9]

Too many Christian couples mistakenly state that they have this "equalitarian marriage" when really they are saying they are "equal before God." The "equal before God" ought to encourage this "equalitarian relationship," but too often all that means is something vaguely theological that is never worked out in the relationship, allowing for the highest good of each. The "equal before God but not equal to find fulfillment in whatever roles will accomplish that" is not the same; in these cases, the husband still rules, controls, and declares the boundaries for what the wife will do and when. It is a relationship where the wife dutifully accepts it as her duty to "submit" and the husband presumes it is his role to "command."

In other instances, there are wives who do work and do pursue careers whose husbands have learned to become short-order cooks, excellent vacuum cleaner commandos, bed-makers, and diaper-changers. These husbands, for the most part, have suffered in silence. This is not "equalitarian" in any sense. This is role reversal, and the two cannot be confused as being the same.

But there are those who are experiencing true "equality" in their marriages without disturbing the rhythm of order and balance or forcing awkward demands on either partner. They are simply carrying out a relationship that fulfills a spiritual oneness and to-getherness. They may not call it "equalitarian," but they do call it "Christian" — and rightly so.

Again, there are too many men who do keep their wives "cor-ralled" at home. But these have a false sense of their role as husbands and as men. On the other hand, men who have that spiritual sense of value become just as excited by their wives' accomplishments as they do by their own and are more than willing to share with them in their pursuits. Men like Doug who have wives of such talent as Midge — or even wives with less talent — welcome that "middle ground" where both of them can feel fulfillment in the freedom of choosing roles that fit.

> Equalitarian marriage has the potential of a far richer and more satisfying form of committed relationship. It emphasizes the commitment to the relationship and to the growth of each person, rather than a giving up of one's personal freedom. It is the sort of commitment that leaves each one free to become as fully human as he or she can, to engage in activities, both work and play, that interest him or her, and to be free to exercise whatever attitudes and tastes come naturally without any par-ticular definition as to whether they are masculine or feminine. The commitment, in other words, is both to the development of the two individuals in the relationship and to the relationship itself. It must be a constantly renewed commitment.[10]

It would seem that such an "equal though different" approach to marriage is not against Scripture. The Bible does not outline any exact relationship, nor does it expand on its principles to cover all of the changes that may occur in human relationships over a period of time. The one principle that does stand as an unchanging base for all relationships is the value of the individual. The one thing that makes Christianity unique is that, by the power of Christ, men and women

are transformed from attitudes of selfish assertiveness and dominance to mutual concern for each other's highest good.

Therefore, the changes in society with regard to the need for
men and women to become more "equalitarian" in their marriage
relationships is not a contradiction of Christian principles if it means
promoting the highest fulfillment in the other. But if Christian
marriages are to weather the pressures of these changes in society,
then there must be more understanding of this value-centered
relationship over against the dominance-independence struggle
that still prevails in far too many households.

Meanwhile, the Scriptures do not refer at all to the man-wife
relationship except in the "submission" and "love" clauses. In
Ephesians 5:21 Paul said, "Submitting yourselves one to another in
the fear of God." The verse applies to the church at Ephesus, but
there is the value principle as it should apply to the body of believers
in general. It is a two-way street, however — a submission to each
other for the other's highest good.

From there Paul goes on into the specifics of man and wife in
verse 22: "Wives, submit yourselves unto your husbands, as unto
the Lord, for the husband is the head of the wife, even as Christ is at
the head of the church and he is the Savior of the body." And then, of
course, verse 25 says, "Husbands, love your wives even as Christ
loved the church, and gave himself for it."

A "submitting" wife is not a "deactivated" wife, even as submission to God does not cancel a person's talents or gifts or intellect or
capacity to work. Paul is expressing what is a sense of divine government over the entire body of Christianity in terms of *order;* but
he is not implying that this cancels the necessity of human relationships that seek the highest good of the other. This is the mistake
some Christian men make in interpreting their role in marriage, and
it is the presumption of too many wives who are convinced they have
more to give than a one-dimensional role in the household. A person
submitted to God is one who has many roles to play in life, as he or
she has the gifts to fulfill them. In like manner, it is not stretching it
to state that a wife "submits" to her husband in terms of his need for
order and continuity in the home. That same fulfillment of order and
continuity works as well for her own sense of balance and stability.
Yet though her primary God-given role may be as a wife and mother,
she has the freedom in Christ to find other roles around that will

fulfill her as a woman and complement her husband. Doug's desire for order and continuity in the household, then, did not put him out of line in terms of this divine government principle; and Midge's need to find new challenges outside the home did not make her derelict. However, it is a question of balance, and the "equal but different" marriage must find that in keeping with this scriptural principle.

In like manner, a husband does not "love" his wife by enslaving her and bringing her to total submission which means denying her the pursuit of various other roles. Even as Christ as head of the church does not force upon His own a one-dimensional role, but "has given gifts unto men" to be used, so the husband displays his love for his wife in terms of helping her use all of her capacities for good.

Midge needed a warning about too much freedom, something the feminist movement is so prone to espouse, because it was removing her from the home where her primary fulfillment was centered. She was moving inevitably toward being a totally independent, self-assertive wife, ignoring the value Doug had as a man and ignoring his need in terms of order.

Adam and Eve illustrate this in their "different though equal" situation. Eve, apparently deciding to do her own thing, to be totally independent, took it upon herself to make the choice that would destroy both of them, a choice which she felt was hers alone to make. With that act, she cancelled the "different though equal," the "equalitarian" relationship and took upon herself a free and self-assertive role with regard to that tree and the fruit that hung on it. This was a revolution against the submission-love principle in terms of the highest value being placed on the other. The disaster that followed is a grim epitaph on the failure of an ideal and perfect union of a man and a woman.

Those who state that Paul's writings were applicable only to the culture of his time with regard to the role of women as "weaker" and thus do not carry all that weight today should also reckon with the lesson of Deborah and Barak (Judges 4).

In the cultural context of the Old Testament a woman was not considered useful other than as a bearer of children and carrier of wood and water. Roles of authority and prominence went to the men. And yet Deborah was given the office of prophetess, one who actually took the position of judge over Israel at that time. The armies of Sisera, king of Canaan, ruled Israel with a strong army and "nine hundred chariots of iron." When Deborah was officially recognized as prophetess, she called Barak, a he-man general, and told him that the Lord had ordered him to fight against Sisera.

Was God deliberately creating a role reversal here? How could a woman command a man in a culture that would consider such a thing as next to death? And yet that he-man did not protest, but came to her for his orders. And here is a remarkable statement of his: "Barak said, 'If you will go with me, I will go; but if you will not go with me, I will not go!'" (v. 8).

Here was a case of "equal though different." Deborah, a woman, was commanding a general, a man, who had the skills to combat the enemy, while she had the presence of God to assure his victory. And this man, instead of feeling demeaned in being ordered by a woman as cultural sensitivity would have imposed, actually solicited her help, that divine presence she had that made her a prophetess of God.

Deborah's sex role moved from that of a subservient woman, destined by men to be of little value, to a position of power as *God made her so*. Barak pushed aside all cultural taboos about women at that point and *yielded himself to her*, not because as a woman she had such a powerful sex role, but because the *presence of God was with her*.

What this says is that the male-female role as dictated by cultural norms, whether by sociologists, church leaders, or writers for feminine revolution, is totally irrelevent to God. Deborah did not lord it over Barak, but it is significant to note that she did accompany him to battle, and Barak won. And Barak, in his victory, did not write his own victory song praising his own manhood; actually it says that Deborah and Barak wrote the victory song *together*, a united song of praise to God for what each had accomplished in their specific roles. Each served a role complementing the other. Deborah did not lose her God-given womanhood in that role, and Barak did not lose his God-given masculinity. God kept the order intact, and that is what "equal though different" is all about.

"Equal though different" is probably the only proper ground upon which marriage can survive the strains of a society going through drastic change. It is the only way to prevent the destruction of either man or wife in the marriage bond and to neutralize the entrenched minds who insist on their "own rights" as man and woman. It is the only way to allow a man his leadership role, without which he feels lost and lonely, while at the same time allowing the woman to find outlet for her God-given gifts.

Doug and Midge will find this level, because they have built an honest communication and sharing with each other. Their separate desires will complement their lives together even as they pursue different avenues for fulfillment aside from their responsibilities to each other and the home and children. Many of their outlets will converge, and they will work together in them. Doug had to finally make this point clear to Midge, not on the grounds of his manly role as leader or that domestic housework was not his responsibility, but on the basis of his own needs and values that he hoped Midge would recognize in her own desire to be out in the job market. In so doing, he checked that slide to a dangerous role reversal which could have ended in disaster. As the two of them worked it out, coming to a new sense of each other's needs and allowing for those needs to be fulfilled around the divine government principles of order and continuity, the submission-love principle was not violated.

What every woman should know is that a man is not so egocentric that he cannot be flexible in terms of what his wife needs for fulfillment. A woman should also know, however, that by nature he cannot abide the loss of continuity, stability, and that sense of rhythm that says to him, "All is well." The old adage, "a woman who wants to keep her man's love should learn to keep his home first," is not altogether archaic. There can be an "equalitarian" relationship, as many Christian marriages have proven. Men must learn to adjust to it and accept it out of love for their wives. Wives must learn to avoid the abuses that can occur by demanding too much, presuming too much.

But it takes a careful working at, and this is where Midge and Doug, like so many others, must learn again the value of each other *to each other* if such a relationship is to be fulfilling and long-lasting.

> Some people feel that with the steadily lengthening life expectancy for women and men it's unrealistic to expect that very many couples can stand each other, much less enjoy each other, for a lifetime. Certainly it's already true that a lot of people don't. Abraham Maslow on the other hand has found

that in self-actualizing people, love and sex satisfactions improve with the age relationship. Since it is more possible to become self-actualized in a relationship of equality, it seems likely that as more whole human beings, female and male, develop, more relationships of depth over long periods of time will become possible.[11]

God does unite and bind two people together for life. If it is to endure, and it can, two people must attune themselves constantly to each other. This is not to be presumed. It is something to be aware of, and it demands an understanding of each other in the total communication process. But what is *communication?*

10.

OF NOT SAYING
WHAT HE MEANS
OR NOTHING AT ALL

"Do you want to go or not?"

"Ummm?"

"The concert . . . go or not?"

"I dunno . . . what do you want to do?"

"You bought the tickets a month ago," she says, a little exasperated now. "What did you have in mind when you did that?"

"I'm not sure . . . maybe I thought it was a good idea then."

"And now? Do I get dressed or do I stay as I am?"

"What time is the concert?"

"Seven forty-five."

"Ummm."

"What?"

"I said . . . ummm."

"That means what? Go or stay?"

"I'm not sure yet."

"When will that mean one thing or the other? Or shall we forget it altogether?"

He yawns, turns another page of the newspaper.

"We got time yet."

"For what? There is supper to be eaten, showers to be taken, clothes to be selected, a baby-sitter to be called, kids to be fed . . . and it is now 6:30. I don't think you *want* to go. So can I presume that?"

"Huh? When did I say that?"

"You didn't," and she has now burned the hamburgers. "But I take it from your present posture of immobility and lack of evidence of great enthusiasm that you are not particularly interested. All I need is a simple yes or no. You paid $6.00 apiece for those tickets. If you don't care about that or the concert, tell me now before I ruin this supper altogether. Can you do that?"

"You want to go?"

Thus endeth the supper, the conversation, the concert. Yet at 7:35 they are racing across town for the auditorium and the concert. She is now in considerable disarray, lipstick on crooked, hair slipping out of the hasty combing, mascara smudged over one eye. She is "silently infuriated," and he is now concerned with that silence and keeps asking, "What did I do wrong?"

It was really in what he didn't say or do, not in what he did, though the final decision to hit the concert like a bolt out of the blue has never set well with any wife, no matter how patient. Many a wife has put on those silences of simmering indignation over a husband's apparent inability to say what he thinks, feels, or wants. Of course, the issue here may be a minor one. The concert will undoubtedly soothe ruffled feelings and correct the misunderstanding, provided the orchestra is not playing Wagner, the musician of war, with a lot of cymbals banging and drums rolling. Yet many a couple has sat through such concerts, church services, or social evenings in silence, unable to surmount the barriers that a lack of communication erected.

Someone has said that there are no "minor" communication crises between a husband and a wife. Each small item adds to another small item until there is ultimately a breakdown in the communication process. Earlier in this book a Christian lawyer pointed out that the hours outside of bed are critical to those which are to be experienced in the sexual relationship; which means there is a lot more at stake in these "little crises" than one imagines. If there is an inability or even refusal to communicate what is meant, felt, or inferred, the intimate areas of the marriage suffer. The best of marriages can run into these communication traps, and the wife will often complain, "He doesn't hear me." Or, "He doesn't listen to me." Or, "I can't get through to him."

In an "equalitarian marriage," where both are seeking to develop and encourage the highest experiences of fulfillment in the other, communication is absolutely necessary. A marriage centered on the value of the other must be centered in "expression" — which means, besides words, the ability to interpret certain signals or signs from the other as indication of a positive or negative to the issue in question.

Communication in its simplest form means to share, to give and receive, and to impart something to another. But in a marriage, communication takes on an even greater importance, because human emotions are at stake. And human emotions are the tinder that can set the fire going in a hurry. In a marriage, communication is to convey as accurately as possible what the feelings are, the emotions, the *specifics* of those feelings. It means conveying *exactly* what is meant by the words or the mere inflections, or even the "ummm."

Wives have confessed that their greatest frustration in their married lives is not in sex or in their husbands' abilities to provide or even protect, but in "his not saying what he means." In some cases wives complain that "he doesn't say much of anything." Others say, "His words are filled with sound and fury, but signify nothing."

Their complaints may be justified, or they may be indications that the woman does not understand her man well enough. In any case, if there is this resentment over a lack of proper communication, the marriage may move on to shaky ground. If either one cannot interpret what the other's needs or desires are, then a slowly widening gap emerges. Each must know what is important to the other. That man in the case history earlier in the book who wanted a cup of coffee in the morning was wrongly interpreted as carrying on empty banter. Actually he was really trying to communicate to her that he wanted her to share breakfast with him, that he needed her company before he started out for the job so early in the morning.

Family service research director Dr. Dorothy Fahs Beck has established this series of specific husband-wife communication problems:

1. mutual suppression — the silent couple;
2. one-sided communication — one spouse withdrawing and the other demanding;
3. stilted or intellectual communication, which operates as a defense against feeling emotions;
4. indirect or devious communication, as through third parties — friends, relatives, children;
5. silence by one spouse intended to frustrate the other;
6. communication limited to quarrels and angry scenes;
7. communication by physical "acting out" in an effort to get through to a nonresponsive spouse.[1]

Too often couples expect their love to cover for this lack of communication in the everyday decision-making or simple exchanges about values, life, and self-needs. Love does cover a great deal of misunderstanding, and that must be emphasized. But it does not replace the need for each party knowing what the other feels, thinks, or even dreams. These expectations that say love conquers all wind up as false expectations, and it takes time to recover from the illusion. Some people don't.

However, a woman needs to know that a man's failure to express himself adequately on all issues that pertain to his life does not constitute a stubborn refusal to do so. Not all men are talkative beings; not all men are at ease expressing their deepest feelings in the kind of phraseology that makes sense. Some men protect certain areas of their inner world because they are caught in that myth that says masculinity begs that a man maintain that private world and not "lay it on his woman." And there are some communication situations that the man withdraws from because he is afraid. His own sense of inability to articulate feelings, or a sense of embarrassment in that the revelation of what he feels constitutes a weakness in him are just two.

In *The Male Machine,* Festeau commented on this point.

In the realm of emotional support, husbands, for the most part, do not give what they get. First, a woman is more likely to be open about her feelings, so the man doesn't have to work at prying them out. More important, he is less likely to make an effort to understand her feelings and needs. Such an effort would require a conscious expenditure of his own emotional energy especially if she is upset or confused and her distress is in some way connected to him. This is something men have never learned to do. Staying calm and controlled is also easier if one doesn't get involved . . . nothing contrasts more sharply with the masculine image of self-confidence, rationality, and control than men's sulky, obtuse, and often virtually total dependence on their wives to articulate and deal with their own unhappy feelings, and their own insensitivity, fear and passivity in helping their wives to deal with theirs. This, more than anything else, disillusions women about their men.[2]

For instance, some men are happier with a wife who does not demand a lot of talk or assurances about their love; some men are content to be with their wives and know that a simple "ummm" or "uh-huh" is perfectly okay and that the wife accepts him for that even if it doesn't say much. Many women have learned to interpret an "ummm" or a "uh-huh" as contentment in their men. So, then, something was definitely communicated that probably wouldn't come out if he was asked to define a feeling at that point.

Lobsenz and Blackburn state that there are several "musts" in a marriage if a healthy communication is going to be developed: 1) "The ability to trust another person in an intimate relationship is probably one of the most important elements in effective communication."

This could mean that the wife who must constantly have her husband demonstrate his love for her or who insists he tell her he loves her again and again during sexual relations is sowing some seeds of doubt in his own mind. On the other hand, a wife who does not need those expressions in the sexual arena and is, contrarily, willing to listen to his fears about his adequacy, is going to build in him a confidence to share more of himself. This, then, will allow her to share more of her own feelings.

2) Another important element of communication is "the ability to accept the validity of another person's feelings, even though they may seem foolish or superficial."

A husband who finally says he's "scared" to go to the doctor is opening an area of his masculinity that is closely guarded. To be frightened of a doctor or a hospital stay is to confess to "weakness" and thus to a "feminine" trait. The X factor is taking over the Y again. The wife who scoffs or laughs and says, "Don't be such a baby!" has driven a wedge into the communication process that will be difficult to remove. A man who is hurting or ill and is unsure what is causing it feels threatened because it affects his leadership and puts his wage-earning responsibilities on the line. He fears more than anything the possibility of being sidelined, becoming a cripple, or being forced into a "non-manly" bedridden posture. Even the best of Christian men face the same issues with the same trepidation. Some try to take it stoically and manage to hold the false image in place. Others want to express their fears about it and receive some assurance from the wife. Mostly they want to know, from their wives, that it is not wrong to feel that way. If they can get that affirmation they are going to open up more and more of the areas of life that need to be shared.

3) Finally we need "the ability to give and receive nonverbal signals that communicate as surely as words . . . which conveys feelings by tone of voice, gestures, facial expressions, even bodily posture."[3]

The man who is slouched in his chair reading a newspaper before supper may be trying to say to his wife, "I don't want to go out tonight, okay?"

Perhaps the man who couldn't make up his mind about going to the concert really did not want to go. He was tired after a tough day. He felt relaxed, and he wanted the evening in that chair more than anything else. Each time he asked her if she wanted to go or not, he was in fact hoping she would say she didn't, thus supporting his own feelings. The reason he did not come out with it and say he'd rather stay home was that there was $12.00 on the line (which she reminded him of) and also the fact that he felt she needed a night out to break up the routine of her hours at home. If she had read his signals properly rather than nagging at him about giving her a "yes" or "no," and had said instead, "Look, let's forget it tonight. There'll be other concerts. Maybe we can give the tickets to some friends. There's still time," she would have dropped a blessing on that man.

Or take the man who stares intently at his wife in a Bible study after she has announced she will ask her husband to interpret the significance of number seven in Deuteronomy. He is trying to tell her something — "Don't do this to me! I am not a Bible scholar! I don't know where Deuteronomy is. Don't put me in this position!"

Often a wife doesn't understand why her husband will embrace her without warning, especially in front of the children. (Nothing wrong with that; in fact it is healthy for the kids.) She will push him off and say, "There's a time and a place for everything!" What that husband is reaching out for, many times, is some sense of assurance. He may be sensing his job is on the line, and with this he realizes a growing loss of control that goes with the fear of failing. The need for the embrace is his need for a touch from the one who is a symbol of continuing faith and trust and love, regardless of what happens to his job. If she does not read that signal and says, "You're embarrassing me!" she will drive him back into his lonely world of private fears that will eat away at him. Many men who are sexually inadequate with their wives will reach out in this way where sex is not demanded, hoping that the wife will respond in kind, thus assuring him of her unconditional love.

Women do have a great responsibility in learning just what levels their husbands feel most comfortable on in the communication process. Some men, for instance, are so tired at night that another social evening is almost too much to bear. When his wife has already accepted another invitation and pushes him into it — because she has been home all day and needs the outlet — he may find himself spending an evening where his own power to communicate is completely impaired.

For instance, the case of Frank W.: After months of heavy socializing, there came the night when Frank, after long hours on the job, was just about out on his feet. After three hours of trying to "talk intelligently" to other guests and not doing too well, the dessert was finally served. Since this was an after-dinner social, it was Frank's first opportunity to sit down and ease his weary body. He sat in a rocker and held his chocolate eclair topped with a mountain of creamy lemon-custard fluff, hunching forward to keep the plate in his lap. It was time to pray. On that night, the man who prayed took considerable time invoking God's intervention in the affairs of men; half-way through Frank began to doze. And just as the final "Amen" sounded, Frank's head fell forward, and his face plopped smack in the middle of that mound of rich, colorful gooey topping. When everyone looked up at a decorated and confused Frank, there were gasps and some uncertain laughter.

At that point, a wife either comes to the rescue or drives her man deeper into his sense of shame and demolishment. She can drag Frank out by the ear with apologies to the hostess, as if he were a little boy still unable to feed himself properly, and thus create a long-lasting breach in the communication process; or she can, as this wife wisely did, pick up on that horrible moment and say lightly, "Well, that's my Frank; he has never been able to wait for the 'Amen' before imbibing!" The attempt worked. The good-natured laughter that followed eased everyone's tensions. And Frank, cleaning himself off a minute later, could laugh with them. He was, in fact, saved from a very embarrassing moment.

It takes a sensitive wife to determine the right words to go with the feelings of her husband in that moment. And many a wife has to learn not to drag an already tired husband to social upon social when his abilities to cope are not really there. Communication sensitivity then would have her saying earlier, "Frank, I am not so sure I am up to going to the Smiths tonight. Shall we take it easy and watch TV for a change?" A man who can get that kind of reprieve when he feels he needs it is not going to have trouble communicating with his wife or appreciating her.

Sometimes marital communication breaks down because the wife does not have a verbal or wordy husband. Because he may not be articulate, she will take charge in social gatherings, making up for his lack. Many a man has sat in such gatherings while his wife did all the talking for herself and for him. As this continues, his own sense of self-image begins to diminish. His ego mastery is being threatened. When someone turns to him and says, "Frank, I heard you had some water in your basement — "

"Nothing at all," she chimes in quickly. "In fact, it was simply a wet spot from the sweating plumbing."

A husband may be conscious of his slowness with words. He becomes more conscious of it when his wife declares it by her insistence on boxing him out of the conversational exchange. Such a man knows his wife is nervous about his slowness, and the more the wife covers for him, the more he withdraws and the more resentful he becomes of her refusal to allow him that expression of his own. A husband who is continually being put down in this way will withdraw, not only from public, but from any meaningful expression with his wife at home.

Besides the conversational put-down a man may experience from his wife, there is another area that is equally if not more frustrating. That is the punishment of silence. It is almost impossible for a man to absorb it. A man who is left to try to figure where he might have gone wrong with his wife, who is not given any hint, who is led to conclude finally that the silence means she is preparing to unload on him, is often experiencing a state of desperation. His work, his self-worth, and his self-image begin to crack under it. A man can probably abide anger, even outbursts of false charges of wrongdoing, but never silence. Silence from a wife is eerie to a man; it is threatening. A wife who uses silence as a tool of punishment is treading on dangerous ground, because it breeds all kinds of unwanted monsters in his imagination. It saps his emotional strength, because he must continue to ponder the why of it, and any man drained of his inner capacities to lead is one who truly becomes a bear. When a woman who is normally quite loquacious suddenly withdraws, without explanation, an aura of hostility begins to build in the household. A man feels totally helpless in that situation; the more helpless he feels, the more resentful he becomes. And whatever the woman had in mind by the silent treatment inevitably turns out far worse than intended.

On the other side, of course, a wife needs to know when to talk about certain things and when not to. Men guard against intrusion into certain areas they feel they must keep to themselves. Whether it is right or not, the woman who respects that area or areas is one who will avoid creating unnecessary tension in him and for herself. A man wounded in his job will eventually share that with his wife, but perhaps not immediately. He must have his time of licking his wounds. If he avoids talking about the job, it is a signal to his wife that something may have gone wrong and he is not ready to tell her what it is. Some men cannot express themselves in this area lest it reveal too much of their own sense of fear or anxiety. Men will bluff; they will laugh when inside they are actually hurting; they will scoff at the clouds even when they know a tornado is about to hit. They are deliberately covering those areas they believe constitute their own masculinity. The wife must know or sense, or at least condition herself to know, those attempts at avoidance as an instinctual desire not to show hurt or anxiety, not as a deliberate put-down of her.

In this connection, there is often misunderstanding between husband and wife about what appears to be "avoidance" or "distance." Alice Fleming, in "Making It More Intimate," comments on the problem of either spouse being too busy for the other.

"At the heart of the disagreement . . . is a difference of opinion about marital space," she says, "which is the physical and emotional distance between husbands and wives." She quotes Edward T. Hall, professor of anthropology at Northwestern University, who identified four separate distances at which most people operate: intimate, personal, social, and public.

As already indicated, not all men can handle all four distances the same any more than women can. "While some feel uncomfortable in public spaces (the stage or lecture platform), or social (dinner parties), others cannot endure being close to people, including, quite often those who have the right to expect such closeness, the husband or wife."

"One signal," Fleming explains, "is a preference for closed doors or solitary pursuits. Another is a distaste for displays of affection except in the privacy of the bedroom. In the living room husbands and wives who shrink from intimacy will generally sit at a considerable distance, or even facing away from their spouses. When they are worried or upset they will seldom admit that anything is wrong, much less explain what it is. Yet when these people say, 'Of course, I love you,' they are baffled or hurt when their spouses are not convinced."

Fleming explains that what appears to be "avoidance" is perhaps traceable to a possessive, intrusive mother who has made him permanently on guard against an overly close relationship with his wife. Or "people who have grown up in chaotic or unhappy homes may have developed the habit of withdrawing as a way of insulating themselves from turmoil. A partner may then be reluctant to express personal feelings for fear of being rejected."[4]

So sometimes a husband will work late, or take work home to keep busy, as an escape from closeness or intimacy. And a wife may throw herself into community and church affairs for the same reason.

Too much "distance" building, though, is dangerous. What complicates it is that a wife may interpret it wrongly as being deliberate by her husband or vice versa. A man may withdraw because his wife makes too many demands on him for either intimacy or conversation. At any rate, any man who feels closed in and goes into periods of withdrawal has to be approached in terms of understanding, not interrogation.

Nothing works better than for a wife to bring to the "master," sitting it out in his private study, a tray of goodies to share with him. Rather than demanding why he is "hiding out" or "avoiding me," the sharing with him without demand does more to open up communication than anything else. Food still has a way of neutralizing tension. A man can talk around food and drink, because it gives him a good prop. In the sharing, intimacy is returning, and he does not realize it. After a while he looks forward to those times together, and the wife who has carefully and gently cultivated those moments with him will know the reward of a husband who finally overcomes his problem.

"Marital space" may occur. It happens in the best of marriages. Both husbands and wives must cope with it in each other. But the important key is not to presume that "distance" means a man is less interested in his wife. Or vice versa.

"If they can work toward improving the quality of the time they spend together, and not worry so much about its quantity," Fleming says, "they will have made a major step toward shortening the emotional distance between them."[5]

The fact that Christian couples go through the same crises in communication does not mean that Christianity fails them as a value system. Actually, when Christ does become the focal point of marriage, the possibilities of communication are much more enhanced. A man who now realizes he can talk to God in private about those things he does not feel he can share even with those closest to him is bound eventually to sense a new confidence to open himself without fear to his wife. Most important, he must be encouraged to pray together with his wife, and perhaps only she can lead him to do so. It is true that a man can protect his inner feelings even in prayer with another, but when his wife opens herself in prayer, when she is honest and sensitive about her needs in that way, he eventually will feel the same confidence.

In praying together, the man who may feel distant about his own emotional problems can experience two things: First, he senses he is on neutral ground; he is not forced to open himself directly to his wife about what he calls his private concerns. Yet as he talks to God in her presence he is in essence sharing with her as well. Second, prayer together has a way of creating honesty and openness — if it is more than mere ritual — and builds a certain sense of oneness that a man must have if he is to eventually feel free to come out of his shell.

Then there is the added necessity of joint Bible reading. Too many husbands and wives carry out their own "private devotions," reading Scripture on their own. This private, spiritual and devotional exercise does little to create honesty and trust where it might be shaky. Add to that the fuzzy prayers before meals and the slurred, exhausted jabbering to placate God before going to bed, and the result of that shallow spiritual exercise is for the most part negative.

The Bible is an honest book. It deals with human temperaments and communication problems. It deals with failure and shortcoming. Its precepts are earthly. The Psalms alone capture the human struggles that a man faces every day and provide confession for sin and great shouts of victory as well.

A man might get all of this in his private Bible reading, but to catch the sweep and grandeur, the honesty of communication, with his wife can and has in many cases unblocked a man who has suffered a crippling self-consciousness about his own inability to express himself. A wife, however, cannot force him to any kind of joint exercise that he may feel is threatening. One wife began a two-year process whereby each of them read one promise card to each other at breakfast every morning. "My husband, who guarded against all human emotion to himself, soon began to ponder some of those verses," she explained. "Then he was asking questions. Suddenly the wonder of the biblical record led us to further and more extensive examinations. . . . as much as we had read those passages by ourselves before, and I know he did, suddenly together there seemed to be something of even greater significance. It wasn't long before we were sharing openly and honestly what both of us had locked up inside ourselves for a long time."

For those who suffer communication crises, even as Christians, there needs to be a fresh realization that the Spirit as "Paraclete" — one who comes alongside — is still the major healer in those baffling times of what appears to be avoidance. Distance is far more quickly and permanently bridged by His official work than by all the exhaustive psychological diagrams or even therapy, though that is not to be totally discounted. Communication is, after all, primarily God's business. The cross is the epitome of God's desire to bridge the communication gap that appeared between Himself and man in the

Garden. When Christians ignore this concern of God for His own, they are shortchanging themselves. It is true what John Powell said in his book, *Why Am I Afraid to Tell You Who I Am?*: "To understand people I must try to hear what they are *not* saying, what they perhaps will never be able to say." The human capacity to do that is limited, vastly limited. To know what a man "is *not* saying" can only come through intimacy that is spiritually cultivated. He who probes the inner mysteries of man, who knows what man is, He alone can reveal that and He alone can finally take away the fears or reticence a man senses in his protectiveness about what he communicates.

However, the mundane must always be faced. God does not provide magic formulas for removal of all the mental and emotional blocks that can interfere with the communication process of a marriage. He does provide the confidence to share, the love to accept, the willingness to give and take. That in itself is surely enough. But beyond all that, there will always be corners and pockets of mystery; there will always be times when it is best to be silent, best not to ask, best not to wonder, best not to nag, best not to presume, best not to push for explanations.

Christian marriages are beset by the same tumults as non-Christian, and some of these are not quickly, perhaps never, answered conclusively through the spiritual application. But where two people have a trust of each other rooted in God, they at least have a *sensitivity* that recognizes when and when not to make an issue of communication or noncommunication. When Paul told the Roman Christians, "Let us follow after the things that make for peace" (Romans 14:19), the words were directed to individuals as well as to the church in general. More than anything else, a man wants an aura of peace in his home, a peace that does not demand of him what he cannot give. He senses, at the same time, his responsibility to make his home peaceful, to give contentment to his wife, to see that his children know safety and security and some measure of happiness in life.

Even in that he may seem to be creating tension instead of peace, but only because, very often, the wife may be expecting more from him than she should. For the woman who continually feels that "he never tells me he loves me" could be misjudging the strength of his love. Some things are better "felt than telt." In any case, "telling" is not always that easy for some men. Performance is the one way in which his own communication of that love comes about. Because he cannot demonstrate it, articulate it, sing it, coo it, or lavish it with chocolate and flowers does not mean he does not love her.

A personal advertisement in the *Dallas News* said: "Alice, I love you more than duck hunting. Dave." Laughable? Maybe. A far cry from what a true communication of love is supposed to be to a woman? Maybe. But maybe for Dave this was the only way he could verbally communicate it, and in the communication he was saying that his love for duck hunting still came second to his love for his wife. For a good many men that is the only way they can truly indicate their feelings. The wife who doesn't catch the truth of it, even in that rather feeble way, has not come to understand her man at all.

Love is what ultimately removes communication blocks. But it is not always love that is surface, soapy, or demonstrative. There comes a time when both husband and wife find that kind of love that goes beyond the purely sensual or demonstrative.

A. H. Maslow, in his book *Motivation and Personality*, talks about "self-actualized" people. This means people who have achieved a full development in their emotional lives. Most important in Maslow's concept, though, is that self-actualizing people attain that "ability to be accepting."

Lloyd Ahlem, in his book *Do I Have to Be Me?* commented on Maslow's theory this way:

> In the love relationships of self-actualizers, there is a great desire for psychological as well as physical intimacy. Secret languages and gestures develop between couples that only they understand. Responses toward each other tend to be spontaneous, free from defenses, the tyranny of roles and inhibitions. One can be himself completely. No energy is wasted worrying about one's self-presentation or in suppressing anxiety. So accepting of each other are these partners that they become a single personality, yet each is fully developed. Each allows his partner an irreducible, autonomous integrity. Yet each feels the needs of the other as his own.[6]

This is that mysterious, beautiful love called *agape* in the Greek, which is referred to throughout the New Testament. It is the way God in Christ views His own, accepting the totality of the

human person He has created and regenerated in both the failures
and the successes. It is a love that is given without thought of return.

> Unlike reciprocal love or even mutual love, agape love is a "no
> risk" relationship. You never get to the place where the love has
> been discontinued because of some fault of yours. You are
> never reduced in the eyes of God because of some failing. You
> can't lose this love. God always continues His love toward you
> in spite of any trait or deed. There is never a time or place
> where you cannot begin again.[7]

Paul was speaking of this love in Romans 8:35 when he said,
"Who can separate us from the love of Christ? Shall tribulation, or
distress, or persecution, or famine, or nakedness, or peril, or
sword?"

"What man needs most is the redeeming experience of agape
love," Ahlem continues. "We are all subject to the human failures
that damage every one of us. No one is free from some hang-up. But
no experience of failure removes us from the possibility of knowing
the highest love of all."[8]

Sometimes a man can't communicate to his wife as he should all
the things he feels. Often he is afraid to do so. But agape love, if it is
nourished by the wife toward him, accepting him regardless of how
much he can say or demonstrate, can bring the fullness of reward in
the end.

Joyce Brothers, in her article "When Your Husband's Affection
Cools," summed it up very well in her advice to those wives who feel
they are short-changed without this constant demonstration in
communication.

> Marriage is not just spiritual communion and passionate em-
> braces; marriage is also three-meals-a-day and remembering to
> carry out the trash. Indeed, love is not the whole business of
> life, and a man who has the woman he wants may be forgiven if
> at times he seems preoccupied with his work. Remember:
> being "taken for granted" can be a compliment. It means that
> you've become a comfortable *trusted* element in another per-
> son's life.[9]

But time inevitably marches on. The heat of summer slowly
gives way to the snap of fall. The struggles to adjust to spring, to
grow up in the July and August nights, suddenly brings on the first
shock of frost in October. The morning a man wakes up to the chill

can either send him scrambling back to the blankets for the duration or else challenge him to put his feet over the bed and rest them on the cold tiles of reality.

Even though communication no longer remains such a problem, even though he has now found his level and she has come to understand him, he is about to enter a puzzling, depressing, and almost frenzied moment in his life. It is a danger point, even for the Christian man, which he may not recognize for what it is. It is the point at which he and his wife may face the greatest test of all.

11.

THE MIDDLE YEARS —
DEAD STOP
OR FULL STEAM?

O the days that are gone by,
  O the days that are no more,
When my eye was bold and fearless,
  And my hand was on the oar.

— Aristophanes

"Am I thinning out?"
"Where?"
"My head, where else?"
"Not anywhere else that I can notice — "
"But . . . but look! It's . . . it's showing!"
"A lot is showing lately — "
"I mean my scalp . . . my scalp is showing through!"
"Maybe you're growing an extra head, how's that?"
"I'm going bald," he says dismally.
"So is the eagle. Take heart — "
"You don't care?"
She smiles. "There are worse things going on in the world to all kinds of people."
He tries to smile too. But during the day he won't smile. He will begin to feel some panic. He is in his forty-sixth year now. His

children are in college. Whatever he had yet planned to accomplish in life, he won't. Whatever dreams he had, he can forget them. He now begins to examine himself closely before the mirror every morning. Sags, pouches, protrusions.

"Look! A lump!" he says, charging out of the bathroom after shaving, waving a long index finger behind his ear.

"Yesterday it was chest pains," she says laconically. "The day before it was a loud crack in both knees when you crouched to do your RAF exercises, which means arthritis — "

"Will you look?" he pleads. "Feel that . . . right there — "

She feels it. "Yes," she sighs in that tone that sounds like the final diagnosis. "The fat is going to your head, old boy!"

It can be funny, and the wife who can keep it on that level will save him a great deal of suffering. But the man knows, nevertheless, that this is all a beginning of a change for him, a turning of the corner that can either be destructive emotionally or, if he can pull it together, a grand and glorious rush for the wire. It is not much of an adventure at this point. For all he notices is "age." This realization is even more compounded and reinforced by the fact that he notices a slackening of his sex drive. He begins to gulp alfalfa, bone meal, and wheat germ, but his sexual powers are not coming back as they once were. He takes to reading all the sex manuals he can in hopes of finding the clue, hiding away in the stack rooms of the library so no one will know. He doesn't sleep well, and lying awake he sees visions of a horrible disease consuming him, of wheelchairs, hospital beds, and the slow shrinking away to inevitable death. He begins to wonder about his job, how long he can hold it against the pressure of those younger. He begins to have doubts about his own spirituality, about God, faith, and the Bible. The quietness of the house is eerie. It is a tomb. The silence is like a grave. The sounds that once echoed off these walls, the sounds of children's laughter, squealing with delight, the "happy birthday" choruses . . . only echoes now, all gone. Now it's only the two of them. The world has become a grand subtraction table for him. And he then rightfully asks: "Is this all there is?"

It need not be "all there is," of course. But at this point for the man there is a shock wave rolling over him that shakes his sense of self-worth and self-image. It's an insult. Age is a mockery to strength, to manliness. It is not something he can laugh at. He wants to fight it, but is helpless to know how. It is not something to resign himself to; rather, it is something to hate, to resist. For many men the realization of sore limbs, aching backs, and changing anatomical design is illogical and a mean joke, not a sign of "maturity." Who wants to be "mature" if sex diminishes, breath comes hard, muscles tighten, and the end of the day comes with the ten o'clock news?

And so he refuses to accept it. Many men would rather fight than submit. They hurl themselves into their work with a frenzy. They buy flashy clothes, sporty cars, and try to get attention from the younger girls in hope of getting validation for their "eternal youth." *Time* magazine (8 March 1968) described the man who fights the inevitable: "Along in his forties, the American male often plunges into strange fits of depression. He wakes in a sweat. He stares at the ceiling. His once-bright ambitions creep past like beaten soldiers. Face it: he will never run the company, never write that novel, make the million. He feels fat and futile; his kids are taller than he is. He ponders some escape. Should he dye his hair, have an affair, get divorced, quit his job? But how can he sacrifice that pension, that company-paid insurance? What new employer wants him? What girl?"

Let there be no mistake: Christian men can suffer the same shocks of middle age as non-Christians. Age is no respecter of persons. Emotional reaction to it can be as bizarre with a Christian as with his non-Christian peer. One Christian leader who came through it confessed, "I woke up one morning and realized for the first time that I had put twenty-four years of my life into the pastorate . . . and right then I wondered what good had I done in all that time. What was the point of it all? I had no more edge on life or age or death for those years than my pagan neighbor across the street. Except maybe he had more to show for it — more money, property, and prestige." For this man, it was his wife who rescued him from sliding off into a hopeless preoccupation with those thoughts. She was smart enough to detect the signs of it in him in the same way she detected her own "change."

What women need to understand is that men can go through their own "change of life" experience even as they themselves do. Helen C. Smith, in her article "The Male Change of Life," quoted Dr. Helen Ruebsaat on this point: "Chauvinistically, most men, even most doctors, are reluctant to face up to it, but males can go through something very much like the female menopausal process. And while women are emotionally prepared for their change of life, men are rarely prepared for theirs. The effect can be traumatic . . . for the man, his family, his fellow workers, and, in the case of a politician, the public."[1]

Smith also quoted Dr. Luciano L'abate, marriage and family counselor and clinical psychologist, who referred to this time as "middle age crisis" and added, "It's one of the more severe crises a man can face, but if it's conquered, his marriage can be a very satisfactory one, or if not, he can make hell for everyone."

In the same article, Dr. Jack Balswick, associate professor of sociology at the University of Georgia, explained it further: "It's a time of questioning the rat race. Our society has put such emphasis for men on achievement-centered goals and we have glorified the 100 percent silent man who doesn't know how to express love and gentleness. This is a hindrance to the deep-sharing communicative relationship that nurtures marriage."

Not all men go into a nose dive, of course. Many manage to cope with reality without a hitch in stride. But those who go through varying behavioral changes in their attempt to try to accept it need sympathy and understanding in the same way that the wife expects it for her time of change. Handling the man who now begins his fight to overcome is not always easy. A woman must be careful not to allow off-beat behavior to be classed as "childish" or to describe that behavior as an "embarrassment to me." A wife must recognize that her husband has found the worm in his own apple, and the psychological jolt that goes with it can be shattering and demolishing.

Frank Hotchkiss, who did a study on the men in the city of Los Angeles, summed up how devastating the awareness of middle age can be.

> The middle-aged, who have the skill and energy and capability to do the most, often shy from the real tasks, deny their imagination and intuition, and settle for dreary compromise. It is the hectic, shortsighted, striving of the middle-aged that is most filled with vanity and which too often constitutes the wasteland of our lives. Thus it appears that youth is not wasted on the young but rather that capability is wasted on the middle-aged.[2]

In any case, the man who comes to awareness of his middle age and who reacts by becoming "hectic, shortsighted or striving" need not go through any crippling self-destructiveness. Again, a wife is the best balancer, the one who can best reason with him, if she has the patience out of love for him. But she must recognize it for what it is; if she does not, she may, instead, become one more force bending him to defeat.

A man's first awareness of age comes from his waning sexual power. His peak of sexual power is in his twenties, and it will run on through into the forties. The lowest point is in his eighties. But during the middle forties and on to the fifties, a man can sense he is losing the power that he once had at his command. In this awareness a man can become testy, panic-stricken, and depressed. He will become more so if his wife reminds him of it.

The man may now begin to look for remedies both from his doctor and from health food dispensers. "You can tell a man's age by taking a look inside his medicine cabinet," someone once said. The difficulty is that the more tranquilizers that are taken, the more repressed he becomes sexually. During this period he may also experience hot flashes, sweats, generalized weakness, loss of energy, poor concentration.

In many cases the loss of sex drive can be traced to chemical changes which can be adjusted by medical therapy. The wife needs to know that. Often psychological counseling will help a man gain reassurance about himself. The wife needs to know that as well. It is not a permanent condition, but more important, for the wife, there must not be the conclusion on her part that his loss of sex drive is her fault. What hurts, however, is that sometimes he will blame her for his failures; he does not know where else to place it. A man does not talk or cannot talk to others about his "change of life" or his loss of sexual power; and if he won't see a counselor, then he will continue to turn the thing over in his mind and arrive mostly at the wrong conclusions. No man has the bravado to tell another man he is "going through male menopause," so he will rationalize his abnormal behavior as normal. He will ignore the signs if he can and continue to drive himself to prove they are all wrong.

At this point, then, he becomes highly vulnerable. Not only is his sexual universe shattering, but he cannot find his sense of identity as a man. So he begins to complain more. He eats too much. He gains weight and yet insists on swimming five miles a day to prove he has lost nothing of the power he always had. He becomes talkative or doesn't talk enough. He may even question his spiritual values, pursue bizarre spiritual experiences, or withdraw completely from involvement in spiritual exercises. No man reacts the same to this time of crisis; for the woman it can bring a sense of uneasiness, even fear, because she is never certain what it means or what it will finally produce.

It is tragic that it is at this point in life when marriages seem to crack the quickest — a time when a man is fighting to find himself, and when his wife is not sure what he is fighting. The wife fears one thing above all else — especially in his preoccupation with his waning sexual powers — that he will become unfaithful, have an affair. Her desperation to please him sexually, coupled with his lack of power to return it, precludes in her mind that he is tiring of her. A wife who fears this in her husband, who feels that "this is bound to happen eventually," that inwardly she "always knew that he, like all men, would sooner or later practice infidelity," creates an atmosphere that complicates rather than relieves those fears.

The Christian man, however, despite his inner tensions sexually is not that far out of control — not yet. A Christian man is governed by two principles of loyalty: his wife and his God. He, by the sensitivity he has spiritually if for no other reason, is unable to carry out sexual affairs outside his marriage, because he knows he could not live with a broken commitment. He knows that commitment to his wife and God are symbolic of a relationship that is enduring — to break it is too big a price to pay. No man wants to face the internal conflict of the disorder of that broken commitment.

Wives often smile at that and say, "You don't know my husband." Maybe. But perhaps she does not know him either then. The term "commitment" is too often interpreted as a pledge to something or someone that must be kept whether one wishes to or not. There is too much duty in it, and duty is not a proper credence for faithfulness. And it doesn't have enough power to hold a man from extramarital indulgences. However, commitment is born out of love. It is not separate or distinct from it. A man's commitment out of love, as said earlier in this book, means he gives himself, all that he is, to that one person, because to him there is no one else. When the years wear down the word "love" and there are fewer episodes of electricity and sky rockets that once marked his youth, love is seen as growing into commitment. It is not that love is less, but that it is now reinterpreted in terms of the ongoing, continuing oneness with that woman. Commitment is not duty; it is a deep desire to protect that woman from hurt of any kind. In committing to her, the man commits something to himself and to God, something deeply woven into his emotional and spiritual fabric. Therefore, it will not be easily moved, and it will not be easily compromised in a man who has come to value that commitment as a big part of his being a man.

The wife, however, who cannot believe that her man, any man, isn't "out to get it" is doing him a disservice and adding to his problem. The wife who has become suspicious of her husband at this point in his life — and granted she may have reason if she does not understand what is happening to him — when he seems erratic in his personality and life style, has probably been suspicious of him throughout the marriage. But whether she has or not, she now begins to wonder, and with that come seeds of distrust. She may now become more "watchful" of him. She may question him too much as to where he has been, whom he took to lunch, how old is his new secretary, etc. She may even manipulate social gatherings to keep certain females out of range. She becomes tight when he goes on long business trips, presuming he will have a wild time away from her, living out all his sexual fantasies with some other woman.

Actually, all a man experiences on the road most of the time is a deplorable loneliness and homesickness, trapped in a hotel room with its meaningless TV programs and loud plumbing. It's at that moment that he senses his need of his wife more than ever, because the world is suddenly strange, hostile, and sometimes too inviting. He knows he can make mistakes, and the contemplation of that is too frightening. Perhaps those who own no such loyalties spiritually sense no crisis, feel no pressure, take what is to be taken. (Though secular man is not to be judged as necessarily being without morals.) For the Christian man, all the shaking, rattling, and huff and puff of middle age crisis can't jar him loose from the deeply imbedded values that govern his temple. Temptation? Yes. Even the Lord had that. But the Christian husband under temptation is more than the woman thinks he is. He may have fear that keeps him, fear of self-destruction in succumbing. He knows that the road to expediency is littered with broken lives. At this critical point, he wants to grab on to something that has stability, permanence, something or someone who will not change as everything and everyone else has changed. His wife stands as the only consistent and durable element upon whom he can lean for support in this shaky world he has been launched into, the world inside.

A man may think of sex, he may have it flaunted before him — but in the end he refuses it. Depending on the health of his marriage, the honesty of communication there, the sharing of problems, the sensitivity to each other's needs, a Christian man will fight to hold the line in the one area he does not want to give up — his life with God and his wife, the one being symbolic of the other.

Twenty out of thirty men interviewed for this book on the question of extramarital affairs stated they would not compromise their spiritual lives on the basis of sex. Five of them interviewed said it would have to be really a "desperate moment in order to drive me to it" or "the situation at home would have to be quite hopeless." Five others said they saw no problem with it, but admitted that it "would be difficult to reconcile as a Christian" or "I would have to deny my Christianity to live with it" or "if it would help my own sexual life with my wife, maybe." All of these ten who said they might consider it also stated that communication with their wives was not all that good, but hastened to add that it wasn't the wife's fault as much as their own. The pressures of job, travel, and trying to get ahead had cut into home life too much.

The survey is too brief and the responses not broad enough to indicate anything that conclusive about Christian men and extramarital experiences. But all admitted that Christianity was something more than a *system* of belief or a code to prevent breakdowns in marriage vows. It was, in fact, a *controlling force,* as they put it in most cases, which they accepted as the key to their own fidelity. If Christianity is that strong to men, then it can be just as strong in healing all the areas of a marriage where there is fracture; and strong enough, as well, to help a man suffering his middle age trauma to come to a new sense of renewal and to somehow get it all together again. Wives need to know this.

Christian men who do succumb to the pressures of outside sexual encounters — and there are those who do — must live with themselves and with that broken commitment. And it is not as easy on a man as women think. A man has certain territory he wants to protect, and he will do all he can to avoid compromise that would encroach on that territory. Once he does compromise, something is forever lost. The sexual relationship with his own wife — no matter the strength or weakness of it — is one area he is most sensitive about. A Christian man in particular feels that it is the one close, real, genuine relationship that has durability in a world of fragility. Besides, he knows that what he foolishly takes from another woman is not a relationship but an exercise.

Greene put it this way:

> A man, for example, who is anxious about his manliness and driven to prove repeatedly a potency of which he is uncertain may make of the sexual relationship a proving ground for his own identity, rather than a mutual sharing and merging with that of another. Sex becomes a contest in which he wins or loses, rather than a bodily language of relationship through which he may in part come to know, and be known by, the unique mystery of the other. It is as though he was not really free to be in the experience but only to dream about it, talk about it, and analyze it before and after it occurs.[3]

For the Christian man who allows himself the indulgence there is the awful knowledge that the Christian ethic has not proven itself in him or by him; his own manliness has not been strong enough to prove itself, and he has introduced an element of destructiveness into his own life and into that home that he needs for coherence and order. Few men deliberately court such disaster for just one moment of indulgence. Those who do are never the same again in terms of their own self-image in God and in their relationships with their wives.

Often there is a confusion concerning the terms "fidelity" and "infidelity." Andrew Greeley clarified them somewhat when he said:

> Fidelity in any relationship is a permanent commitment to "reach out," a promise to persist in efforts to transcend the barriers and the distance that separate one from the other, a firm resolve to maintain effort in sustaining and developing the relationship no matter what difficulties and trials arise . . . it also means a commitment to increasing sensitivity to the other. . . .
>
> Infidelity is not the same as adultery, at least in the primary meaning. Infidelity means quitting, a giving up on any aspect of a relationship when there are still possibilities remaining. . . .

The reason why we Christians are faithful in our relationship to one another is that Yahweh is faithful to us. And in the sexual imagery of the prophets Jeremiah and Ezekiel, Yahweh emphasizes that even though we whore with false gods, he will not see other people. We might turn our backs on him but he will never turn his back on us. We might be unfaithful, he will never be unfaithful. The Good News that Jesus brought was in effect a renewal of that old covenant . . . when a Christian man and woman remain faithful to each other, they are manifesting God's or Yahweh's love to the world. . . .

Whether premarital or extramarital sex is sinful is not nearly so important as whether Christianity can sustain the positive demands of faithfulness. If it can then the question of sex outside of marriage can be answered within a religious context. If it cannot, then the church is simply one more ethical or moral lawgiver with nothing unique to add to human customs.[4]

What Greeley seems to be espousing is that man remains faithful to his wife only because God shows His faithfulness to him. Actually, though, what Greeley is suggesting is that a man who senses the deep commitment of God to him, even in his failures, can understand more fully the beauty and fulfillment of like commitment to his wife. It means coming to grips with the reality of the value of the person beyond the inadequacies of that person.

The fact is that Christian men daily prove their fidelity as being a spiritual matter and not simply a legislative one. And as long as a man hangs on to the spiritual value that puts the highest premium on his life partner and realizes it as being a protective, life-giving principle given by God, he will remain faithful. The rewards for that are the very elements he needs: order and coherence in his world and within his home and his family. Fear and guilt are not enough to hold a man in check; only this higher positive value rooted in the spiritual can do it.

At the same time, infidelity is often mistaken by wives to include the appreciative look a man gives to another woman, whether it be her legs, hips, breasts, or any other thing of beauty that delineates the feminine. Men, who all their lives up to the middle age crisis, have been scolded, sermonized at, accused, or penalized by preachers or wives who consider all such looks as "lust" and who have never known freedom or trust may be pushed to a costly sexual crisis at this point. Or, as in some cases, men who are unable any more to tolerate the pressure of a condemnatory wife or culture will rebel with drastic acts to give vent to what they believe is purely normal and innocent in that appreciation of feminine beauty. Man has reflexes in this regard that he cannot explain himself. To have to explain them is only complicating it further.

Man's appreciation for feminine beauty is not the same as lust. A man knows the difference *most* of the time. There is a fine line between the two, and it is the man alone who must interpret his feelings before God. No one on the outside, even his wife, can do so unless he confesses his specific lustful feelings. Man is a mystery when it comes to the sexual, and even he cannot always determine exactly when a look is in effect lusting. The church has given very little help on the matter either, content only to emphasize the word "lust" in the catalog of the "thou-shalt-nots." It is cruel and unnecessary punishment to lay on him thoughts or feelings regarding other women which are not there, or to make him feel guilty about a look. "How *long* he looks is probably the only signal I have," one wife said, and maybe that is the only measurement after all.

At any rate, a good, faithful man of God feels that he wants his life committed to God and to his wife without blemish. The wife who will trust him on that is going to be the key to helping him through the difficult times he experiences emotionally when he may skate too close to the edge on these matters. But if she suspects him, thinks the worst of him, she will hurt him. That will only support his fear that he is hurting and failing her and prove that something is really happening, that something has in fact gotten out of control, that he is not capable of negotiating the trauma of this "change."

This does not mean that some of the best spiritual men — and women for that matter — don't make mistakes. But a spiritually sensitive man is quick to recognize it for what it is and put it right. Judgment, in any case, is God's province alone and is not the prerogative of his peers or even his spiritual leaders. That man must travel the trail to mourning, repentance, and restoration alone with God. Any man who will go on that journey, if he must, is a man worth keeping. The woman who refuses to accept him when he has made that journey does not understand how much he hurts, how much he loves her, how much he is willing to pay to keep her love above anything or anyone else. And in so doing, she will cut herself off from a man who has exhibited the epitome of character.

What this all says, perhaps, is that this period in a man's life, this time of confusion during which he fights to regain or discover his identity, can tax a wife to the extremes. She cannot know that in his hours of quiet desperation he needs her more than ever to be his strength, to give him assurance that she is not loving him less for what is happening to him, much of which she experiences herself in her own way. This is a time, of course, when the years have worn down the cement of what has been the love relationship of the earlier years — they are now two people totally familiar with each other, and this can breed complacency and even indifference.

As the wife needs a husband's understanding for her time of identity crisis in middle years, so he needs hers. Here again is where that *agape* concept of love is the only answer. This "accepting" is essential, this loving without looking for return favors; this loving that will continue to affirm a man and declare him worthy of her love, despite his faults, is what will hold the marriage together. (And it applies both ways.) A man and a woman must both draw on it, use it, apply it, hold on to it as the most precious treasure of all. As Ahlem put it, in this kind of love "you don't need defenses, polish, morality, intelligence, religiousness. You need a person. When you find Him [Christ], who is love, He may lead you to these virtues. But they are no substitute for Him."[5]

A man needs not only the assurance of *agape* love from Christ, but the same from his wife. He is fully aware of what is happening to him, of the strange forces that have locked him into such a bitter inner struggle. He knows that his behavior is as painful to her as it is embarrassing to him. At that point he is most vulnerable. At that point he must have assurances that the woman in his life who counts the most *accepts him* in spite of it. And he must know that she accepts him and loves him, not because he will hopefully straighten out and fly right as it were and crown her queen of all, but because he belongs to her, and that possession is the most precious thing to her.

If he negotiates this test from youth to middle age, it will be largely because the one closest to him has suffered through his fears and panicky moments with him with patience and understanding. If she corrects him, it must be in the spirit of love, not in the spirit of reprimand. He is not fully in control of his psychological and spiritual forces, and she must know that. He would not choose to experience this, even as she would not choose her own comparable stormy hour. But he does not know how to appeal to her for understanding, because he does not want to admit he is experiencing anything that has to do with "change" or that he can't cope with the devastating realization of his waning powers. Though he may dress in the latest fashions straight out of the teen-age commune and drive a Porsche, and though he engages in youthful athletics that could kill him, just to prove he has "still got it as a man," he needs his wife as never before to help him through. Only the woman in his life can "read" him at this time; and only she, if *agape* love is central to her life, can help him negotiate the trauma of it and keep him from self-destructiveness.

But middle age is not the end of the line, nor does it have to be a continual struggle to find new identity. It is not a period of regression to childhood, nor is it a time to head for the rocking chair.

Balding, changing body contour, loss of energy, and sexual changes do not signal that a man is finished. It can be and should be the "prime of life." A man has to find that, even as his wife must.

It must be remembered that Abraham settled down in Haran and was quite content to let the middle years (he was 75 then) be lived out in the quietness of that familiar place. God called him once to come out, but Abraham did not respond. Like many middle-aged men, perhaps he felt incapable of rising to any new challenges. God had to call him again for "the land that I will show you." Abraham then obeyed, and he began a journey that was to bring the greatest fulfillment of his life (Genesis 12).

Moses had spent forty years of his life running cattle and by then was well over sixty when God confronted him in the burning bush. Moses spent some time arguing with God about going down to Pharaoh to tell him to let the Jews go to the Promised Land. All the arguments were rooted in a sense of total inadequacy; who knows, perhaps Moses felt his time had passed, that the task called for someone younger (Exodus 3,4). But when he finally received the seal of God that he was to go in the renewed power of the divine, Moses went. And for him it was the beginning of an adventure unprecedented in his life up to then.

It is the same today. Composers, artists, generals, writers have done their greatest works during the "prime years" beyond fifty. The Christian man, rather than succumb to the shocking reality of his age, is in a position to make all his years count for something even greater. God is in reality calling out a new Abraham and a new Moses perhaps, because such men have proven themselves, have attained a wisdom that is necessary for new ventures, and are the best qualified to do the new work ahead.

Robert J. Havighurst, in the book *Aging in Today's Society*, suggests some points to help those in middle age — men and women — to become more positive about what their years can mean. But often it takes the calmness and patience of the wife to get a man to see these things:

1. "VALUING WISDOM VS. VALUING PHYSICAL POW-ERS" — "Havighurst suggests that middle age is the period in which to substitute thinking and the wisdom that comes from maturity for physical satisfaction." Face it then. It is not a time for sexual marathons or great expenditures of energies in other directions. It costs too much. Havighurst is suggesting that one can accomplish a great deal more during this period than earlier because mental effort concentrates on "things that are really important." As physical powers decrease, respect the limitations; make the other powers work to fulfillment and satisfaction. Sometimes that simple truth can turn a man from his charade at being more than he is and his fruitless fight against the encroachments of age.

2. "EMOTIONAL EXPANSION VS. EMOTIONAL CON-STRICTION" — In short, now that the children are gone and the house feels "eerie," this is not the time to allow the emotions to dry up. It's time to expand to new friendships. Emotional isolation is the danger of middle age — a man may simply want to give up and withdraw to his favorite chair and let the world go by. Now both he and his wife will either begin to slide off into narrow, uneventful, monotonous final years or they will reach out to new individuals, new opportunities. A man, in particular, needs to get his mind off himself, off his sense of lost opportunities, of the world running out from under him. Finding new friendships among those of his own age who may be feeling the same can rejuvenate both he and his wife, perhaps as nothing else can.

3. "MENTAL FLEXIBILITY VS. MENTAL RIGIDITY" — This means getting rid of mental inactivity. A man stops thinking

when he senses it doesn't count for much any more. The "fat literally goes to his head." To do so is to deprive others of a mind that has accumulated a conditioning that can work for church or society. A Christian man can and should now begin to reach out to those areas of church life that need a fresh mental view of the problems. Some middle-aged men who have had early retirement have gone off to mission fields in a totally new dimension for the benefit of many. To be mentally rigid is to be fixed, frozen, and this means intellectual death. Change the reading. Change the patterns so that the mind can get new exercise. If the man won't move that way, the wife should drive him to it until he finally catches the spark.

Havighurst concludes by saying, "Just before the prime of life, when a man or a woman is working most efficiently and meeting the demands of life most successfully, it is true in a paradoxical way that he is least free. . . . He has little freedom . . . people can be happy and free and young in spirit in their middle age and for a long time afterward if they do some personal stock-taking and planning for this period in their lives."[6]

No one knows how long a man will suffer through his middle-age trauma. That depends on how soon he lays hold of the practical suggestions and spiritual values available to him. The church can help too by giving as much attention to the forties, fifties, and sixties as they do the teenie-boppers. Churches who plan mixed-group programs (the older with the younger) periodically are helping immensely to bridge the generation gaps and give the older a new sense of youth and enterprise. Too often the gray-haired, pot-bellied, bifocaled people in church audiences have no sense of continuity within the spiritual life of the church. The battle is for the young, not the old. Sermons are geared to the young, vigorous visionaries. The older are left to find what they can from each other. Some do. Some don't. Too many just drift. In this lack of interest on the part of the church leadership for the "wisdom and maturity" of those in middle age, some find a confirmation of their own inner fears. It ought not to be.

And yet, as already emphasized, a man in his middle years is now ready to give of his best to his church, his God, his business, his family, and his community. All that has gone before has been conditioning for this greatest moment of all. If he won't be used by those who should use him, then it is up to him to find where he himself can work for the good of others and himself.

One day this man will no longer worry about his age. One day he will have passed through the long night of frightful disorientation about himself, his self-image, his bodily and mental capabilities, his sexual powers. How he comes through is greatly dependent on his wife's patience and willingness to recognize what is happening to him and her encouragement in helping him resist the attitude that life ends because the body and its energies change.

That man, if he gets through without blowing apart, will have disproved F. Scott Fitzgerald's declaration: "There are no second acts in American lives." There are second acts. And third. And who knows how many more? The Christian man, above all, should know that God puts no stock in age. He may find it hard to realize at the beginning of the fall and winter of his life, but the fact is he can.

For the woman in his life, who waited out the night of storm with him, there is also the reward of sharing that glorious second act with him.

12.

THE CHRISTIAN MAN —
THE EXTENT OF
THE DIFFERENCE

He's a good man, I'd say that for him,
and a true Christian every inch of the way.

— Cervantes, *Don Quixote*

On the night of their twentieth wedding anniversary, Doug and Midge Masterson celebrated. It was not his plan, but hers. He came home at five and found the table beautifully decorated — candlelight and Chinese food.

It was a delightful evening. Though celebrating the twentieth is not quite the same as the big one at twenty-five, Midge Masterson declared this twentieth as a "milestone." And so it was perhaps. As the saying goes, "If two people can make it the first twenty years, chances are they will go to fifty, God willing."

For Midge, it was her way of communicating that the twenty years were worth it. For Doug, it was a reinforcement to him that somehow he had managed to give to his wife all that made for her happiness and contentment. In the soft glow of those candles, in a room made mellow by their exchange, she gave him a card that read:

> His life was gentle, and the elements
> So mixed in him that Nature might
> stand up
> And say to all the world, "This was
> a man!"
> — Shakespeare

"Was?" he said playfully, though moved.

She shrugged. "I want to say it now while we are in our right minds and not afterward, or when you are gone. . . ."

He read further, for underneath those famous lines from the master of literature was another: "To you who have lived Galatians 5:22 for twenty wonderful years!"

Earlier in this book there were cases referred to where husbands and wives were in such tension that intimacy was no longer possible. To them, this scene between Midge and Doug would seem bizarre, out of the ordinary, even extraordinary. For them, the marriage union had decayed, allowed to atrophy . . . there was nothing to remember worth remembering, nothing really worth celebrating. Some would go through the motions perhaps, hoping that in a moment of neutrality there might emerge something of value that would rebuild an already broken union.

Doug and Midge are viewed too often as the "unusual" relationship of a man and wife. Or some would say such a relationship is cultivated only in the halls of the famous, the unusually gifted, the tenacious, the ones "blessed" above the common herd.

And yet for Doug and Midge there are twenty years of adjusting and readjusting behind them. There is a record of stormy days and stormy nights as well; times of disagreement, times of quarrel, times of withdrawal, times when their relationship felt the pressures of the same contrary winds as any other.

But for Midge it was the learning about her man that counted in the end. For Doug it was the learning about himself as she helped him to learn that carried him through the years they now have found sweet to celebrate.

The tragedy is that not all women can celebrate any given year in genuine interest with their husbands. Few can write any famous lines to declare their love or what life has meant with their men. For these women, perhaps it is preoccupation with lesser things. For them, the time will come, when it is too late to say it.

For others, there is nothing to be said or celebrated, because their lives have been lived too fast, detached from each other, following separate tracks. Anniversaries come and go with automatic gestures drawn from what is proper rather than from love. They have taken each other for granted. Only the shock of death of one or the other will bring the jolt of the reality of time wasted, of mysteries never probed, of hours spent in a strange stand-off, each refusing to dig deeper than human chemistry demanded or gave.

For others, no celebrations of genuine affection occur, because each partner is still a mystery to the other. They have come to accept each other as necessary partners in a compact with life and even with God. To separate is a stigma. To go on is to prove something, if nothing more than that there is some way to manage a life together even if all the necessary ingredients are missing. For these there is no fruit and hardly celebration.

For Midge, through the candlelight, there is much to recall and remember of these twenty years with Doug. The times he brought laughter for her sorrow; and the times when he could not, being so bent by sorrow himself, he rose to what laughter she tried to give him; times of quarrel, yes, but always he would be the one to make reconciliation and soothe her fears about such differences by quoting the old sage Terence, "The quarrels of lovers are the renewal of love."

In the twenty years together she has come to know his weaknesses as he has hers, but in the end he came to recognize them in himself, and in that was strength; in him was the wild bent to competitiveness, the will to win; there were also, though, the days of honest confession when he would admit that "there is more to life than winning."

Doug learned as much from his wife about living as he taught her. It was in his willingness to be taught, to share, when the man in him — the traditional, mythical part of him — resisted such counsel from his "woman."

There is nothing extraordinary about Doug Masterson. He has no special gift to make a marriage go, no great secret to the relationship of the working parts. He is a quiet man, what history might even call "an uneventful man." He climbed no mountains in those twenty years, never sailed a twenty-foot ketch around the world; he broke no records, made no headlines. There was nothing of the swashbuckler in him, no Rhett Butler of *Gone with the Wind*, no great romantic image, no man of really great accomplishments as men call each other great.

He is a chemist. He works with Bunsen burners and test tubes, and he does his work well. For that he takes home a check every Friday, and that is the extent of his professional life. He would like more — to find new formulas, to make life better through chemistry. But he knows he may never do that. He is content in what he is doing.

Yet he is a man people know. The barber knows him because he tried to entertain a little boy who cried all through his haircut.

The neighbor across the street knows him because he cried with her when her son was reported killed in Vietnam.

A lady motorist still remembers him from the night she was stalled on the expressway in a storm. She remembers his stopping to help, getting soaked while he fixed her flat.

His boss knows him well and treasures him for his precision in his work, as well as for his steady, stabilizing influence on those who work with him.

The manager of Seven-Eleven knows him and shakes his head in some bewilderment even yet as he thinks of his coming back to the store to return fifty cents too much that he received in change for a five.

The kids on the block, many of whom have grown up and gone on to high school, remember him as a man who threw a football rather poorly, but who loved the game and helped them to love it too.

His fellow church members know him, not for any great gift of preaching or teaching or witnessing, but because he was always there for the necessary "common work" — washing the walls, painting, driving the church bus.

Doug Masterson is not conscious of these things on this twentieth anniversary. But his wife is. She knows, because she has taken the time to know. He is not a perfect man. She knows that too. And he has come to know it in himself, and that is the greatness of any man beyond all other accomplishments. She helped him to know himself, because she took the time. Now, however, his imperfections are swallowed up in the gold that endures from his life, that which has come from a man who wants to give as much as get.

That is why Midge Masterson can say with John Milton's verse:

> So dear I love him that with him all deaths
> I could endure, without him live no life.

Many women cannot rise to so glorious a statement about their husbands in life — maybe not even in death. To many women, men like Doug Masterson exist only in the idealistic dreams of naive coeds or confirmed but frustrated spinsters. For those who miss such men in their married years, it may well be, as this book has tried to show, because the wife has never discovered him.

If Doug Masterson is what he is, it is not simply through the sheer desire to be real or through the tenacity of a wife to help him be that way. If he has arrived at some semblance of manhood that has diversity and strengths in many dimensions, it is not that he is composed of different elements than other men.

Doug is a Christian man. Does that make a difference? If so, how much of a difference?

In these pages Christian man has been seen as one who suffers the same pressures, problems, and conflicts over his self-image as his non-Christian peer. The problems of winning, sex, communication, and the stresses and strains of two people living together are just as present for the Christian as the non-Christian.

Let it be said in all fairness that there are non-Christians who are good husbands, many of whom have found themselves, many of whom share celebration with their wives for the years together. At the same time, there are Christian men who have not yet learned to live the virtues they espouse and are yet on their journey to know the truth of what all of it means in terms of a wife and family. Such is the nature of the flesh that creates contradictions. That failure, however, does not negate what God can give to a man and is ready to give.

When Paul wrote in Ephesians that Jesus had broken down the wall between Jews and Gentiles by His death and resurrection, he also stated in chapter 2, verse 15, that the purpose of it all was that he "thus fused us together to become one new person, and at last there was peace" (LB).

Earlier, in 2 Corinthians 5:17, he said, "Therefore, if any man be in Christ, he is a new creation; old things are passed away, behold all things have become new."

As obvious as it may appear, and though it does carry a point of absurdity, it bears emphasis that God does not automatically, in His redemption or regeneration, make the brawny man into a brainy one or vice versa; a "new man" through His creative act is not one who has been suddenly stripped of his manhood, his personality, his need to win, or his sexual capacities or drives. He does not make a eunuch out of a healthy sexual man, nor does He make a traditional Valentino out of a man who may not have all the sexual powers in the world. God does not grow hair on bare chests, give a new set of biceps, make a genius out of a man with an average IQ.

The point of this exaggeration, however, is to say that women who eagerly yearn for their husband's conversion spiritually in order that he might experience a revolution biologically, emotionally, or in personality are presuming too much of God. Women who hope Christianity will make their husbands more pliant to their wills, more willing to accept role changes (or even hopefully that they will no longer be hooked by Monday night football) are victims of excessive and misguided expectations.

Of course, Christ in a man does affect the totality of that man in every dimension to some degree. A stormy man does come to know peace; a dominant man does experience the need for more consideration of his wife's needs and desires; an insecure man can know some real measure of security in Him; and an overconfident, self-sufficient man can realize more clearly that he needs those closest to him in order to negotiate the road to greater fulfillment.

But the woman needs to recognize that these are the blessed by-products of the major thrust of God's act of new construction in a man. What Christ does in making a "new man" is, first of all — and most important — help him to shed the myths that hang on him in terms of how he should *express* his manhood. The myths that man must be dominant over the woman, that he must be all-masculine and deny any feminine traits within him, that he must *perform* to prove himself, that he is basically a sexual animal and therefore has the right to be assuaged whenever he has the urge — these are what Christ deals with first in a man and what He really changes in him. Christ actually gives man his true sense of identity, replacing the false facades man has felt he has had to wear from the year one. A man set free from having to live those myths, to conform to the traditional, universal, cultural norm that all men are men in certain ways or they are not, is a man now free to allow himself to emerge as he truly and uniquely is. And that emergence may be distinct from other men, but now he feels no uneasiness or condemnation in that distinction.

Second, once he is free of the myths, Christ then gives that man the necessary, missing elements that enable him to function in closer harmony with his wife, his family, even his peers. When Paul wrote in Galatians 5:22, "The fruit of the spirit is love, joy, peace, longsuffering, gentleness, goodness, faith, meekness, temperance," he was talking about what Christ gives to a man to bring him to a dimension of complete manhood. These are not feminine traits; they are the fruit of godly character.

Natural man, of course, pays little attention to them because to him they *are* feminine. But that is also why the natural man will lay his hand to a weapon to deal with another man rather than using the entreaties born out of these spiritual values. That is why such a man may cheat on his wife with no sense of compunction, make his home a hell on earth, and "run his own ship his own way." Such a man is forever crippled in his command of life — no matter how successful he is in other realms — because he is unable to effect the healing and restoration in the fragile elements that make up his life.

But every man, though he ignores spiritual values, is drawn to them in the end. Inwardly a man sees in those values the critical means for survival. There must be love in place of hate; joy in place of sorrow; peace in place of strife; longsuffering in place of impatience; goodness in place of self-centeredness and selfishness; gentleness in place of character assassination; faith in place of distrust; meekness in place of arrogance; and temperance in place of gluttony.

That man who, confronted with the wonder of these attributes, lays hold of them in faith comes to realize this is the heart of God, epitomized in His Son, Jesus Christ. The "new man" in Christ realizes then that he has these new values within himself, that they are active, not static, and that when allowed to work give him stature which is far more important than status. If he is locked into the myths of manhood as previously noted, he can only perform in a limited way within these boundaries imposed upon him. But with

the character of God within him, by His Spirit, he can now respond
to life and its challenges and most of all to people — certainly to his
wife, to his children, even to his peers — in ways that are constructive, not destructive. God's Spirit within a man not only gives him
the tools with which to build, but also the eagerness to do so. Here is
the secret to enduring relationships in marriages, families, and even
friendships.

But that does not mean he lives all of these traits to the fullest
every day. A Christian man is still human. He may still experience
days of frustration and even anger as the pressures of life dig deeper
and chafe. He may still suffer many of the problems mentioned in
this book, because his human frailty cannot always absorb or lay hold
of the spiritual values and channel them properly.

Nevertheless, he now has within him a spiritual understanding
that tells him there is a way to mend broken relationships, to find
peace with others, to rebuild the torn-down structure of marriage
and family. He knows now that there is a better way to deal with the
changes around him and within him, that he is not a hopeless victim
of those changes. He knows now that he has within the power to
change his own weaknesses and help those who suffer them within
his own household. The character of God, then, is the genius of God
through Christ to provide the base from which a man can view
positively himself, the world, and those closest to him. It is in such
an atmosphere of positivism, spiritual positivism, that a man rises to
his proper destiny — to be a man who is a healer, a builder, a
peacemaker, a communicator of all that is truly life and truly beautiful.

This is why Doug Masterson is known and will be long after he
has left the scene, not only by his wife but by those with whom he
has even the briefest contact.

This is the kind of man who can answer the great, probing,
demanding question of Shakespeare in *Othello:*

> Is this the nature
> Whom passion could not shake? Whose
>   solid virtue
> The shot of accident, nor dart of chance,
>   Could neither graze nor pierce?

Yes. This is the kind of man who can and is the answer to that
question.

Every woman should know that her man can rise to this new dimension of manhood even as she can rise to the new dimension of womanhood. As long as God continues to rule His universe and works some new creative act every day, there can be one born every minute.

Let the warning stand, however: sometimes men who have possessed this character of God may lose some of the edge, may wander off, may have some of it squeezed from them by the pressures of the day. These, however, may suffer the loss more keenly than it might appear; they are more conscious of the missing, vital link. They will hurt the most, then, until they make their journey back to Bethel. In that journey, they may experience moments of desperation, testiness of temperament, coolness, and even detachment. Before a wife decides that such sudden "madness" is unbearable and looks for refuge elsewhere, she should allow him that journey. She should join him if he will allow her. If not, she can pray that he will complete it. God is faithful. He will never deny what is a genuine pursuit of Him.

For those wives who live in an atmosphere of uneasy truce with their men, perhaps some new knowledge of what makes a man what he is, as outlined here, will give new hope, a place to begin. For those who suffer the bewilderment of these fracturing tensions there is the promise of Milton:

> And ruin'd love, when it is built anew,
> Grows fairer than at first, more
> strong, far greater.

On the human level, perhaps, it is impossible to see that happen, this "building anew" from a relationship that has all the evidence of ashes. But God is still the greatest and most successful arbitrator of unsettled quarrels and tensions that have pervaded the marriage union. It can, as many have proved, begin again with Him.

And for those who have not yet come to know the total wealth of that man in their lives, who have been satisfied with only the surface parts readily visible, now is the time to find the deeper treasures within him. It takes but the touch of that beautiful grace of a woman so endowed by God to unearth them. And in the finding, both become the richer.

Let it be so!

NOTES

Preface

[1]Dietrich Bonhoeffer, *Letters and Papers from Prison* (New York: Macmillan Publishing Co., 1972), p. 198.

Chapter 2

[1]Joseph Epstein, *Divorced in America: Marriage in an Age of Possibility* (New York: Penguin Books Inc., 1975), quoted in "Report from the Sexual Revolution: Trouble at 'Bedrom Olympics,' " *Reader's Digest*, Vol. 106, No. 635 (March 1975), p. 73.

Chapter 3

[1]Andrew M. Greeley, *Sexual Intimacy* (Chicago, IL: Thomas More Association, 1974), p. 17.
[2]Ibid., pp. 19,20,22,23.
[3]Ibid., p. 25.
[4]Ibid., p. 26.
[5]Ibid., pp. 57,58.
[6]Helen B. Andelin, *Fascinating Womanhood* (New York: Bantam Books, Inc. 1975), quoted in article by Barbara Grizzuti Harrison, "The Ooks That Teach Wives to Be Submissive," *McCall's*, Vol. CII, No. 6 (June 1975), p. 114.
[7]Ibid.
[8]Ibid.
[9]Ibid.
[10]Ibid.
[11]Ibid.

Chapter 5

[1]Joan Beck, "Sex, Sex All Around, But Where Is Love?" *Chicago Tribune*, 14 February 1975.
[2]Greeley, *Intimacy*, p. 28.
[3]Ibid., p. 61.
[4]Thayer H. Greene, *Modern Man in Search of Manhood* (New York: Association Press, 1967), p. 106.

Chapter 6

[1]Mary Perkins Ryan and John Julian Ryan, *Love and Sexuality: A Christian Approach* (New York: Holt, Rinehart and Winston, 1967), p. 5.
[2]Epstein, *Divorced*.
[3]Greeley, *Intimacy*, p. 124.
[4]William Masters and Virginia Johnson, *The Pleasure Bond: A New Look at Sexuality and Commitment* (Boston, MA: Little, Brown and Co., 1975), quoted in "Settling Sexual Conflicts," *Reader's Digest*, Vol. 106, No. 636 (April 1975), pp. 84,85.
[5]Epstein, *Divorced*.
[6]Ryan, *Love and Sexuality*, pp. 46,47,51.
[7]Norman M. Lobsenz and Clark W. Blackburn, *How to Stay Married: A Modern Approach to Sex, Money and Emotions in Marriage* (New York: Cowels Book Co., and Chicago, IL: Henry Regnery Co. 1969), p. 87.

Chapter 7

[1]Greene, *Modern Man*, p. 22.
[2]Ibid.
[3]Ibid., p. 30.
[4]Ibid., p. 47.

Chapter 8

[1]Charlotte Holt Clinebell, *Meet Me in the Middle* (New York: Harper & Row Publishers, Inc., 1973), p. 20.
[2]Ibid., p. 23.
[3]Charles Ferguson, *The Male Attitude* (Boston, MA: Little, Brown and Co., 1966), pp. 19,20.
[4]Greene, *Modern Man*, p. 44.
[5]Marc F. Fasteau, *The Male Machine* (New York: McGraw-Hill Book Co., 1974), p. 196.

Chapter 9

[1]Lobsenz and Blackburn, *Stay Married*, pp. 20,21.
[2]Ioid., p. 139.
[3]Sidney Cornelia Callahan, "A Christian Prospective of Feminism," from Sarah Bentley Doely, ed., *Women's Liberation in the Church* (New York: Association Press, 1970), p. 41.
[4]Lobsenz and Blackburn, *Stay Married*, pp. 113,114,115.
[5]Ibid., p. 115.
[6]Clinebell, *Meet in Middle*, p. 49.
[7]Ibid., p. 32.
[8]Ibid.
[9]Ibid., pp. 57,60.
[10]Ibid., p. 59.
[11]Ibid., p. 61.

Chapter 10

[1]Dr. Dorothy Fahs Beck, quoted in Lobsenz and Blackburn, *Stay Married*, p. 66.
[2]Fasteau, *Male Machine*, p. 81,82.
[3]Lobsenz and Blackburn, *Stay Married*, p. 73.
[4]Alice Fleming, "Making It More Intimate," *Reader's Digest*, Vol. 109, No. 654 (October 1976), pp. 155,156.
[5]Ibid.,
[6]Lloyd H. Ahlem, *Do I Have to Be Me? The Psychology of Human Need* (Glendale, CA: Regal Books, 1973), p. 18.
[7]Ibid., pp. 22,23.
[8]Ibid.
[9]Dr. Joyce Brothers, "When Your Husband's Affection Cools," *Reader's Digest*, Vol. 101, No. 606 (October 1972), p. 151.

Chapter 11

[1]Helen C. Smith, "The Male Change of Life," *Atlanta Journal*, January 1976.
[2]Frank Hotchkiss quoted in James A. Peterson, *Married Love in the Middle Years* (New York: Association Press, 1968), p. 67.
[3]Greene, *Modern Man*, p. 102.
[4]Greeley, *Intimacy*, pp. 173,175,178,186.
[5]Ahlem, *Do I Have to Be Me*, p. 35.
[6]Robert J. Havighurst, "Middle Age — the Prime of Life," from Clark T. Tibbetts and Wilma Donahue, eds., *Aging in Today's Society* (Englewood, NJ: Prentice-Hall, Inc., 1960), quoted in Peterson, *Married Love*, pp. 103,104,105.

BIBLIOGRAPHY

Ahlem, Lloyd H. *Do I Have to Be Me? The Psychology of Human Need.* Glendale, CA: Regal Books, 1973.

Andelin, Helen B. *Fascinating Womanhood.* New York: Bantam Books Inc., 1975.

Benson, Robert. *Come Share the Being.* Nashville, TN: Impact Books Inc., 1973.

Clinebell, Charlotte Holt. *Meet Me in the Middle.* New York: Harper & Row Publishers, Inc., 1973.

Doely, Sarah Bentley, ed. *Women's Liberation in the Church.* New York: Association Press, 1970.

Epstein, Joseph. *Divorced in America: Marriage in an Age of Possibility.* New York: Penguin Books Inc., 1975.

Fasteau, Marc Feigen. *The Male Machine.* New York: McGraw-Hill Book Co., 1974.

Ferguson, Charles. *The Male Attitude.* Boston, MA: Little, Brown and Co., 1966.

Greeley, Andrew. *Sexual Intimacy.* Chicago, IL: Thomas More Association, 1974.

Greene, Thayer H. *Modern Man in Search of Manhood.* New York: Association Press, 1967.

Lobsenz, Norman M., and Blackburn, Clark W. *How to Stay Married: A Modern Approach to Sex, Money and Emotions in Marriage.* New York: Cowels Book Co., and Chicago, IL: Henry Regnery Co., 1969.

Masters, William, and Johnson, Virginia. *The Pleasure Bond: A New Look at Sexuality and Commitment.* Boston, MA: Little, Brown and Co., 1975.

Peterson, James. *Married Love in the Middle Years.* New York: Association Press, 1968.

Powell, John S. J. *Why Am I Afraid to Tell You Who I Am?* Chicago, IL: Argus Communications, 1969.

Ryan, Mary Perkins, and Ryan, John Julian. *Love and Sexuality: A Christian Approach.* New York: Holt, Rinehart and Winston, 1967.